SEO 2020
LEARN SEARCH ENGINE OPTIMIZATION
WITH SMART INTERNET MARKETING STRATEGIES

Expanded & Updated

Adam Clarke

Simple Effectiveness Publishing, Publisher.
Cover Design: Simple Effectiveness Publishing.
Production and Composition: Simple Effectiveness Publishing.

Adam Clarke has completed a certificate in the Google Analytics and Google Ads Qualification programs.

SEO 2020: Learn search engine optimization with smart internet marketing strategies.
Adam Clarke
Print ISBN 9781712354889
Kindle ASIN B00NH0XZR0

TABLE OF CONTENTS.

- Link outreach — scaling up high quality link building campaigns.
- Additional link building strategies.

5. Social media & SEO.
- Is social media important for SEO?
- Facebook & SEO.
- Twitter & SEO.
- Other social networks.
- Social media analytics.

6. Web analytics in a nutshell. How to measure your success.
- Why use Google Analytics?
- How to use Google Analytics.
- Acquisition.
- Organic Search report.
- Segments.
- Common web analytics terms explained.
- Call tracking — powerful analytics for every business.
- Other web analytics tools.

7. Troubleshooting common SEO problems & how to fix them.
- What to do when your site is not listed in Google at all.
- What to do when your business is not ranking for your own business name.
- What to do when your rankings have dropped off.
- How to seek professional help for free.

8. Local SEO. SEO for local businesses.
- Why use local SEO?
- How to rank high with local SEO.
- Local search ranking factors.
- Getting started with local SEO.
- Building citations.
- Building reviews.
- Supercharging local SEO with photos and videos.
- Local SEO ranking checklist & essential resources.

9. How to dominate search with rich results. Structured data, JSON-LD, Facebook Open Graph & More.
- What are rich snippets?
- What are rich snippets?
- Why you need to focus on rich results.
- Why use Structured Data and JSON-LD?
- How to get started with JSON-LD.

FREE SEO CHECKLIST PDF AVAILABLE AT THE END OF THIS BOOK.

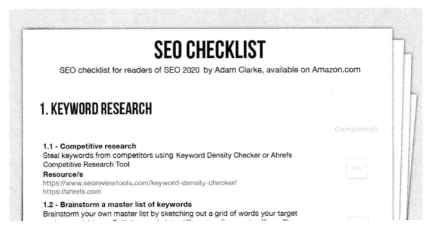

The free 50-point SEO 2020 - SEO Checklist PDF, covering exact steps to improve your website's ranking in Google, is available for readers at the end of this book. Instructions on downloading the SEO checklist PDF are at the end of the book.

INTRODUCTION TO THE UPDATED EDITION.

So, you've picked up *SEO 2020* and decided to learn search engine optimization. Congratulations! SEO marketing has changed my life and it can change yours.

Over 10 years ago, I achieved my first number one ranking in Google for my family's home business. The phone started ringing with new customers every day and I was hooked.

Since then, I have used search engine optimization to grow hotel chains, large international fashion brands, and small family-owned businesses. One thing never ceases to amaze me—the power of SEO as an Internet marketing tool for growing any business. I have grown small businesses into giant companies in just one or two years—simply from working the site up to the top position in Google.

Unfortunately, learning SEO is difficult, sometimes impossible, for many business owners, Internet marketers and even tech-heads.

I have a theory on why this is so...

Sifting through the information flooding the Internet about SEO is overwhelming. In many cases, the advice published is outdated or misleading. And the constant updates by Google make it hard for SEO beginners and gurus alike to keep up with what works.

SEO can be simple and used by anyone to rank at the top of Google, grow their business and make money online. It's simply a matter of having up-to-date information on how Google works, using effective techniques and taking action.

This book has been expanded and updated to cover how SEO works now and likely in the near future. All of the resources and tools have been updated and made relevant for 2020. It includes broader coverage of the basics, and filled with more techniques for advanced users. And due to requests by readers, it has been loaded with more tools and resources to save time and get bigger results.

If you are a beginner, there is a small amount of technical information included in this book. If you really want to learn search engine optimization this can't be avoided. We've made these areas as simple as possible, while providing additional resources, including an SEO checklist, that will speed up your journey to SEO mastery.

If you are an advanced SEO optimization professional, this SEO book covers Google's latest updates, new SEO marketing best practices to refresh your memory, solutions for common technical problems, and new tools and resources to sharpen your skillset — all written in an easy-to-read format, so refreshing your knowledge doesn't feel like a chore.

Whether you're a complete SEO beginner or well-versed Internet marketing veteran, *SEO 2020* covers these areas and makes it as simple as possible to achieve rankings, traffic and sales.

Enjoy.

INTRODUCTION TO HOW GOOGLE WORKS.

You can feel like a dog chasing its own tail trying to figure out how Google works.

There are thousands of bloggers and journalists spreading volumes of information that simply isn't true. If you followed all the advice about SEO written on blogs, it's unlikely you would receive top listings in Google, and there's a risk you could damage your site performance and make it difficult to rank at all.

Let me tell you a secret about bloggers...

Articles about the latest SEO updates, techniques or tips are often written by interns, assistants or even ghostwriters. Their job is to write articles. The majority of blog posts about SEO are rarely written by experts or professionals with the day-to-day responsibility of growing site traffic and achieving top rankings in search engines.

Can you learn from someone who doesn't even know how to do it themselves?

You can't. This is why you have to take the advice spread by blog posts with a grain of salt.

Don't get me wrong. I love bloggers. There are bloggers out there who practice and blog about SEO and do it well. But it has become increasingly difficult to sort the wheat from the chaff.

Fear not. This chapter will disperse common misconceptions about SEO, show you how to avoid falling into Google's bad books and reveal how to stay up to date with how Google ranks sites.

But first, to understand how Google works today, we must understand a little bit about Google's history.

OLD-SCHOOL METHODS THAT NO LONGER WORK.

In the early days of Google — over 15 years ago — Google started a smarter search engine and a better experience for navigating the World Wide Web. Google delivered on this promise by delivering relevant search engine results.

Internet users discovered they could simply type what they were looking for into Google—and BINGO—users would find what they needed in the top results, instead of having to dig through hundreds of pages. Google's user base grew fast.

It didn't take long for smart and entrepreneurially minded webmasters to catch on to sneaky little hacks for ranking high in Google.

Webmasters discovered by cramming many keywords into the page, they could get their site ranking high for almost any word or phrase. It quickly spiraled into a competition of who could jam the most keywords into the page. The page with the most repeated keywords won, and rose swiftly to the top of the search results.

Naturally, more and more spammers caught on and Google's promise as the "most relevant search engine" was challenged. Webmasters and spammers became more sophisticated and found tricky ways of repeating hundreds of keywords on the page and completely hiding them from human eyes.

All of a sudden, the unsuspecting Internet user looking for "holidays in Florida" would find themselves suddenly arriving at a website about Viagra Viagra Viagra!

How could Google keep its status as the most relevant search engine if people kept on spamming the results with gazillions of spammy pages, burying the relevant results at the bottom?

Enter the first Google update. Google released a widespread update in November 2003 codenamed Florida, effectively stopping spammers in their tracks. This update leveled the playing field by rendering keyword stuffing completely useless and restored balance to the force.

And so began the long history of Google updates — making it hard for spammers to game the system and making ranking in Google a little more complicated for everyone.

GOOGLE UPDATES AND HOW TO SURVIVE THEM.

Fast forward 15 years and ranking in Google has become extremely competitive and considerably more complex.

Simply put, everybody wants to be in Google. Google is fighting to keep its search engine relevant and must constantly evolve to continue delivering relevant results to users.

This hasn't been without its challenges. Just like keyword stuffing, webmasters eventually clued onto another way of gaming the system by having the most anchor text pointing to the page.

If you are not familiar with this term, anchor text is the text contained in external links pointing to a page.

This created another loophole exploited by spammers. In many cases, well-meaning marketers and business owners used this tactic to achieve high rankings in the search results.

Along came a new Google update in 2012, this time called Penguin. Google's Penguin update punished sites with suspicious amounts of links with the same anchor text pointing to a page, by completely delisting sites from the search results. Many businesses that relied on search engine traffic lost all of their sales literally overnight, just because Google believed sites with hundreds of links containing just one phrase didn't acquire those links naturally. Google believed this was a solid indicator the site owner could be gaming the system.

If you find these changes alarming, don't. How to recover from these changes, or to prevent being penalized by new updates, is covered in later chapters. In the short history of Google's major updates, we can discover two powerful lessons for achieving top rankings in Google.

1. If you want to stay at the top of Google, never rely on one tactic.

2. Always ensure your search engine strategies rely on SEO best practices.

AUTHORITY, TRUST, RELEVANCE & USER BEHAVIOR. FOUR POWERFUL SEO STRATEGIES EXPLAINED.

Google has evolved considerably from its humble origins in 1993.

Eric Schmidt, former CEO of Google, once reported that Google considered over 200 factors to determine which sites rank higher in the results.

Today, Google has well over 200 factors. Google assesses how users are behaving on your site, how many links are pointing to your site, how trustworthy these linking sites are, how many social mentions your brand has, how relevant your page is, how old your site is, how fast your site loads... the list goes on.

Does this mean it's impossible or difficult to get top rankings in Google?

Nope. In fact, you can have the advantage.

Google's algorithm is complex, but you don't have to be a rocket scientist to understand how it works. In fact, it can be ridiculously simple if you remember just four principles. With these four principles, you can determine why one site ranks higher than another or discover what you have to do to push your site higher than a competitor. These four principles summarize what Google are focusing on in their algorithm now, and are the most powerful strategies SEO professionals are using to their advantage to gain rankings.

The four areas of focus are: Trust, Authority, Relevance and User Behavior.

1. Trust.

Trust is at the very core of Google's major changes and updates the past several years. Google wants to keep poor-quality, untrustworthy sites out of the search results, and keep high-quality, legit sites at the top. If your site has high-quality content and backlinks from reputable sources, your site is more likely to be considered a trustworthy source, and more likely to rank higher in the search results.

2. Authority

Previously the most popular SEO strategy, authority is still powerful, but now best used in tandem with the other two principles. Authority is your site's overall strength in your market. Authority is almost a numbers game, for example: if your site has one thousand social media followers and backlinks, and your competitors only have fifty social media followers and backlinks, you're probably going to rank higher.

3. Relevance.

Google looks at the contextual relevance of a site and rewards relevant sites with higher rankings. This levels the playing field a bit, and might explain why a niche site or local business can often rank higher than a Wikipedia article. You can use this to your advantage by bulking out the content of your site with relevant content, and use the on-page SEO techniques described in later chapters to give Google a nudge to see that your site is relevant to your market. You can rank higher with less links by focusing on building links from relevant sites. Increasing relevance like this is a powerful strategy and can lead to high rankings in competitive areas.

4. User Behavior.

Are users sticking to your content like glue? Or are they visiting and leaving your site faster than Usain Bolt?... How users behave on your site are currently the strongest factors in Google's algorithm. You can take advantage of this by improving user experience — techniques covered in later in this book.

HOW GOOGLE RANKS SITES NOW—GOOGLE'S TOP 10 RANKING FACTORS REVEALED.

You may have wondered if you can find out the exact factors Google uses in their algorithm.

Fortunately, there are a handful of industry leaders who have figured it out, and regularly publish their findings on the Internet. With these publications, you can get a working knowledge of what factors Google uses to rank sites. These surveys are typically updated every second year, but these factors don't change often, so you can use them to your advantage by knowing which areas to focus on.

Here's a short list of the strongest factors in the top 10 search results, according to recent industry studies:

- Direct website visits.- Click-through-rate.
- Time-on-site.
- Bounce rate (low bounce rates are better).
- Number and quality of backlinks.
- HTTPS—security certificate installed on site.
- Overall content relevance and keyword usage.
- Font size in main content area (presumably people find larger fonts more readable and leads to higher engagement).
- Number of images.
- Total social media activity.

If your competitors have more of the above features than yours, then it's likely they will rank higher than you. If you have more of the above features than competitors, then it is likely you will rank higher.

Combine this knowledge with an understanding of the Google updates covered in later chapters, and you will know what it takes to achieve top rankings.

The above ranking factors are from the following industry surveys. If you want a deeper look into the studies, you can browse the full reports by visiting the links below. I also cover the latest updates to the algorithm in the Google Algorithm updates chapter later in this book.

SEMrush Ranking Factors 2.0
https://www.semrush.com/ranking-factors/

Search Metrics: Google Ranking Factors
https://www.searchmetrics.com/knowledge-base/ranking-factors/

Moz Ranking Factors Survey
https://moz.com/search-ranking-factors

HOW TO STAY AHEAD OF GOOGLE'S UPDATES.

Every now and then, Google releases a significant update to their algorithm, which can have a massive impact on businesses from any industry. To hone your SEO chops and make sure your site doesn't fall into Google's bad books, it's important to stay informed of Google's updates as they are released.

Fortunately, almost every time a major update is released, those updates are reported on by the entire SEO community and sometimes publicly discussed and confirmed by Google staff.

A long-extended history of Google's updates would fill this entire book, but with the resources below, you can stay abreast of new Google updates as they are rolled out. This is essential knowledge for anyone practicing SEO, at a beginner or an advanced level.

You can even keep your ear to the ground with these sources and often be forewarned of future updates.

Google Updates by Search Engine Round Table
https://www.seroundtable.com/category/google-updates

Search Engine Round Table is one of the industry's leading blogs on SEO. At the page above, you can browse all of the latest articles on Google updates by a leading authority on the topic.

Search Engine Land
https://searchengineland.com/library/google/google-algorithm-updates

Search Engine Land is another authoritative, relevant and frequently updated publication about everything SEO. An indispensable resource for keeping abreast of search engine updates as they happen.

Moz Blog
https://moz.com/blog

The Moz blog is mentioned several times in this book and for good reason — it's among the leading authority blogs covering all things SEO, and if there's an impending update on the radar, you will catch wind of it here.

KEYWORD RESEARCH. THE MOST IMPORTANT STEP OF SEO.

WHY IS KEYWORD RESEARCH SO IMPORTANT?

Keyword research is the most important step of every SEO project for two reasons:

1. If you rank your site highly for the wrong keywords, you can end up spending lots of time and effort, only to discover the keywords you have targeted doesn't receive any traffic.

2. If you haven't investigated the competitiveness of your keywords, you can end up investing lots of time and effort into a particular keyword, only to find it is far too competitive to rank, even on the first page.

These two pitfalls are often the ultimate decider on how successful any SEO project is.

This chapter will cover how to avoid these pitfalls and how to find the best keywords. First, we must define what a keyword is.

WHAT EXACTLY IS A KEYWORD?

If you are an SEO newbie, you may be wondering — what is a keyword?

A keyword is any phrase you would like your site to rank for in Google's search results. A keyword can be a single word, or a keyword can also be a combination of words. If you are trying to target a single word, lookout! You will have your work cut out for you. Single word keywords are extremely competitive, and difficult to rank highly for in the search results.

Here's some different kinds of keywords:

Head-term keywords: keywords with one to two words, i.e. classic movies.

Long-tail keywords: keywords with three or more phrases, i.e. classic Akira Kurosawa movies.

Navigational keywords: keywords used to locate a particular brand or website. Examples would be Facebook, YouTube or Gmail.

Informational keywords: keywords used to discover on a particular topic. This includes keywords beginning with "how to…" or "what are the best..."

Transactional keywords: keywords entered into Google by customers wanting to complete a commercial action, i.e. buy jackets online.

In most cases, targeting head-term or navigational keywords for other brands is competitive and not worth the time or effort. Despite their high traffic numbers, they will generally not lead to any sales. On the other hand, long-tail, informational and transactional keywords are good keywords for most SEO projects. They will lead to more customers.

HOW TO GENERATE A MASSIVE LIST OF KEYWORDS.

There are many ways to skin a cat. The same is true for finding the right keywords.

Before you can find keywords with loads of traffic in Google, you must first develop a list of potential keywords relevant to your business.

Relevance is vital.

If you spend your time trying to cast too wide a net, you can end up targeting keywords irrelevant to your audience.

For example, if you are an online football jacket retailer in the United States, examples of relevant keywords might be:

Buy football jackets
Buy football jackets online
Online football jackets store USA

Irrelevant keywords might be:

Football jacket photos
How to make your own football jacket
Football jacket manufacturers
How to design a football jacket

You can see how the first pool of keywords are more relevant to the target audience of football jacket retailers, and the second pool of keywords are related but unlikely to lead to customers.

Keeping relevance in mind, you must develop a list of potential keyword combinations to use as a resource, so you can then go and uncover the best keywords with a decent amount of traffic each month in Google.

Following are some powerful strategies you can use to help with generating this list.

1. Steal keywords from competitors.

If you're feeling sneaky, you can let your competitors do the heavy lifting for you and snatch up keywords from their sites.

There are many tools out there created for this sole purpose. A simple and free tool is the Keyword Density Checker. If you enter a page into this tool within seconds it will scrape a list of the keywords your competitor has optimized into their page. You can then use this to bulk out your keyword list.

Keyword Density Checker – SEO Review Tools
https://www.seoreviewtools.com/keyword-density-checker/

While the Keyword Density Checker is a great, simple tool for revealing the keywords your competitors have optimized into the page, another powerful tool is Ahrefs Organic Keywords report. This tool estimates the keywords that are sending the largest amount of traffic to your competitors' websites. The estimates are reasonably accurate and can be a valuable resource for bulking out your keyword lists.

While Ahrefs reports are powerful, they do come at a cost. You can preview the first 20-keywords for free, but if you want more data, they currently offer a 7-day trial for $7, and after an initial trial, monthly billing starts at $99 per month.

Ahrefs – Competitor Research Tools & Backlink Checker
https://ahrefs.com

2. Brainstorm your own master list.

Assuming competitors have been thorough with their research isn't always the best strategy. By brainstorming combinations of keywords, you can generate a giant list of potential keywords.

To do this, sketch out a grid of words your target customer might use. Split the words into different prefixes and suffixes. Next up, combine them into one giant list using the free Mergewords tool. With this strategy, you can quickly and easily build up a massive list of relevant keywords.

Mergewords
http://mergewords.com/

Prefix
- buy
- where do I buy

Middle word
- NFL jerseys
- NFL uniforms
- NFL jackets

Suffixes
- online

Combined keywords
- NFL jerseys
- NFL jerseys online
- NFL uniforms
- NFL uniforms online
- NFL jackets
- NFL jackets online
- buy NFL jerseys
- buy NFL jerseys online
- buy NFL uniforms
- buy NFL uniforms online

- buy NFL jackets
- buy NFL jackets online
- where do I buy NFL jerseys
- where do I buy NFL jerseys online
- where do I buy NFL uniforms
- where do I buy NFL uniforms online
- where do I buy NFL jackets
- where do I buy NFL jackets online
- NFL jerseys
- NFL jerseys online
- NFL uniforms
- NFL uniforms online
- NFL jackets
- NFL jackets online

HOW TO FIND KEYWORDS THAT WILL SEND TRAFFIC TO YOUR SITE.

Now you have a list of keywords, you need to understand how much traffic these keywords receive in Google. Without search traffic data, you could end up targeting keywords with zero searches. Armed with the right knowledge, you can target keywords with hundreds or even thousands of potential visitors every month.

Unfortunately, in recent years Google has restricted access to the data behind Google's search box, leaving us with two options for finding keyword traffic data.

Firstly, if you have a Google Ads campaign running with Google and are already spending a modest amount, then you're in the clear, you can access this info for free in their Keyword Planner tool. If this isn't you, the other option is to use a paid keyword research tool for a small monthly fee, such as keywordtool.io. As a result of Google making search data unavailable to free users, free keyword tools disappeared from the market, making paid research tools the only viable option for finding traffic data for keywords these days.

If you're on a tight budget, then you can sign up for a paid plan with one of the many paid keyword research tools on the market then ask for a refund after doing your research. It's not nice, but it's an option—either way, you need the traffic data behind your keywords otherwise you are running blind.

1. Estimating keyword traffic data with Google's Keyword Planner.

Google Ads Keyword Planner
https://ads.google.com/home/tools/keyword-planner/

As mentioned, to access all the juicy traffic data provided by the Google Ads Keyword Planner tool, you need an active Google Ads campaign running, and must be spending at least a modest amount of money regularly. If this is you, sign in, click on Tools in the top-menu, click on "Keyword Planner" then click on "Get search volume data and forecasts", copy and paste your keywords into the box. Select your country, and then click the blue "Get started" button. When finished, you will have the exact amount of times each keyword was searched for in Google.

Mmm. Fresh data. This is just the kind of data we need.

Now we know which keywords receive more searches than others, and more importantly, we know which keywords receive no searches at all.

	Keyword	Clicks	↓ Impressions	Cost	CTR
☐	[football jerseys]	1,761.27	20,014.10	A$3,036.48	8.8%
☐	[football jackets]	85.57	1,001.40	A$52.36	8.5%
☐	[football jerseys online]	21.28	146.43	A$25.34	14.5%
☐	[where to buy football jerseys]	0.35	5.14	A$1.22	6.9%

2. Estimating keyword traffic data with a paid tool like KWFinder.

KWFinder

https://kwfinder.com/

If you want a research tool with a stronger SEO focus, then you can use a paid tool such as KWFinder. I like KWFinder for its ease of use, relevant keyword suggestions, and competitive data, but you're not limited to this tool — there's many alternatives floating around you can find with a couple of Google searches.

Using KWFinder as an example, after creating an account, simply log in, select the local area you are targeting (i.e. Los Angeles, California, if that is your customer focus), enter your keyword ideas and download the juicy data. Now you can ensure you spend time focusing on keywords with traffic potential, as opposed to chasing after keywords with no traffic and little opportunity for growing your business.

HOW TO FIND KEYWORDS FOR EASY RANKINGS.

Now you need to find out how competitive your desired keywords are. Armed with an understanding of the competitiveness of your keywords, you can discover keywords you can realistically rank for in Google.

Let's say you are a second-hand bookseller and you want to target "book store online." It's unlikely you are going to beat Amazon and Barnes and Noble.

But, maybe there's a gem hiding in your keyword list few people are targeting—maybe something like "antique book stores online."

You have the advantage if your competitors haven't thought of targeting your keyword. You simply have to do better SEO than they are doing and you have a really good chance at beating their rankings. Part of this includes having a large keyword list for your research.

Next, you need to wash this list and separate the ridiculously competitive keywords from the easy keywords no one are aggressively targeting.

There are many schools of thought on how to find the competitiveness of your keywords. The most popular practices are listed below, with my thoughts on each.

1. Manually going through the list, looking at the rankings, and checking if low-quality pages are appearing in the top results.

This is good for a quick glance to see how competitive a market is. However, unreliable and you need real data to rely on.

2. Look at how many search engine results are coming up in Google for your keyword.

Google   football jackets

Q All   🖾 Images   ⊘ Shopping   🖾 News   ⋮ More   Settings   Tools

About 200,000,000 results (0.53 seconds)

The amount of results is listed just below the search box after you type in your keyword. This tactic is common in outdated courses teaching SEO, but completely unreliable.

The reason? There may be a very low number of competing pages for a particular keyword, but the sites ranked at the top of the results could be unbeatable.

3. Using the competition score from the Google Ads Keyword Planner tool.

Don't be tempted. This is a common beginners mistake, and sometimes recommended as an easy way to judge SEO competitiveness for keywords on some blogs, and it just simply doesn't work!

The competition score included in the Google Ads Keyword Research tool is intended for Google Ads advertising campaigns only. It is an indication of how many advertisers are competing for the particular keyword through paid advertising. Completely irrelevant for SEO.

4. Using a competitive analysis tool, such as KWFinder's SEO Difficulty report.

To get a realistic idea of your chances for ranking high for a particular keyword, you need to understand the strength of the pages currently ranking in the top-10 search results for that keyword.

A great tool for this is KWFinder's SEO Difficulty report. With KWFinder's SEO Difficulty report, simply enter your keyword into their tool, click "check difficulty", and it will show vital stats for pages appearing in the top 10.

Of these stats, the most important are Domain Authority, Page Authority, Links, and Facebook Shares... If you don't have high Domain Authority or Page Authority — don't freak out. If your site is more relevant to the topic, you can often nudge your way up the results by focusing on building up backlinks to your page and improving your social media activity, especially if those stronger sites have little amounts of links and social activity on their pages, and are non-specific, generic directory or aggregator type sites.

Next up, if you enter your own website into Ahref's Site Explorer tool, you can see the same stats for your site, and set targets for beating the competition.

Ahrefs – Competitor Research Tools & SEO Backlink Checker
https://ahrefs.com/

Armed with this knowledge, you can hunt around to find keywords with reasonable levels of traffic, weak competition, and set targets for how many links you need for a top listing. You can even find keywords competitors are using, estimates of how much traffic they are getting from those keywords, even where they are getting their links from!

There's many keyword tools and site analysis tools which can be found with a couple of Google searches. Every SEO professional ultimately has a different favorite tool they prefer, the following tools are well known in the field and I often use myself.

KWFinder – Keyword research and analysis tool
https://kwfinder.com/

Ahrefs – Competitor Research Tools & SEO Backlink Checker
https://ahrefs.com/

Moz - Keyword Explorer
https://moz.com/explorer

Moz – Link Explorer
https://moz.com/link-explorer

When finished reading this book, you can work through the keyword research points in the free SEO checklist included at the end of the book, with the above process outlined in a step-by-step approach.

ON-PAGE SEO. HOW TO LET GOOGLE KNOW WHAT YOUR PAGE IS ABOUT.

On-page SEO is the process of ensuring that your site is readable to search engines. Learning correct on-page SEO is not only important in ensuring Google picks up the keywords you want, but it is an opportunity to achieve easy wins and improve your website's overall performance.

On-page SEO includes the following considerations:

1. Making sure site content is visible to search engines.
2. Making sure your site is not blocking search engines.
3. Making sure search engines pick up the keywords you want.
4. Making sure site visitors are having a positive user experience.

Most on-page SEO you can do yourself, if you have a basic level of experience dealing with sites.

If you are not technically inclined, please note there are technical sections of this chapter. You should still read these so you understand what has to be done to achieve rankings in Google, you can easily hire a web designer or web developer to implement the SEO techniques in this chapter, after you know what it takes to achieve top rankings.

HOW TO STRUCTURE YOUR SITE FOR EASY AND AUTOMATIC SEO.

These best practices will ensure your site is structured for better recognition by Google and other search engines.

1. Search engine friendly URLs.

Have you ever visited a web page and the URL looked like something like this:

http://www.examplesite.com/~articlepage21/post-entry321.asp?q=3

What a mess!

These kinds of URLs are a quick way to confuse search engines and site visitors. Clean URLs are more logical, user friendly and search engine friendly.

Here is an example of a clean URL:

http://www.examplesite.com/football-jerseys

Much better.

Take a quick look at Google's search engine results. You will see a very large portion of sites in the top 10 have clean and readable URLs like the above example. And by a very large portion... I mean the vast majority.

Most site content management systems have search engine friendly URLs built into the site. It is often a matter of simply enabling the option in your site settings. If your site doesn't have search engine friendly URLs, it's time for a friendly chat with your web developer to fix this up.

2. Internal navigation

There is no limit on how to structure the navigation of your site. This can be a blessing or a curse.

Some people force visitors to watch an animation or intro before they can even access the site. In the process, some sites make it harder for visitors and more confusing for search engines to pick up the content on the site.

Other sites keep it simple by having a menu running along the top of the site or running down the left-hand side of the browser window. This has pretty much become an industry standard for most sites.

By following this standard, you make it significantly easier for visitors and search engines to understand your site. If you intend to break this convention, you must understand it is likely you will make it harder for search engines to pick up all of the pages on your site.

As a general rule, making it easier for users makes it easier for Google.

Above all else, your web site navigation must be made of real text links — not images.

If your main site navigation is currently made up of images, slap your web designer and change them to text now! If you do not have the main navigation featured in text, your internal pages will almost be invisible to Google and other search engines.

For an additional SEO boost, include links to pages you want visible to search engines and visitors on the home page.

By placing links specifically on the home page, Google's search engine spider can come along to your site and quickly understand which pages on your site are important and worth including in the search results.

HOW TO MAKE GOOGLE PICK UP THE KEYWORDS YOU WANT.

There are many misconceptions being circulated about what to do, and what not to do, when it comes to optimizing keywords into your page.

Some bloggers are going so far as telling their readers to not put keywords in the content of targeted pages at all. These bloggers — I'm not naming names — do have the best intentions and have really taken worry about Google's spam detection to the next level. But it is madness.

Not having keywords on your page makes it difficult for Google to match your page with the keyword you want to rank for. If Google completely devalued having keywords on the page, Google would be a crappy search engine.

Think about it. If you search for "Ford Mustang 65 Auto Parts" and arrive on pages without those words on the page at all, it's highly unlikely you have found what you're looking for.

Google needs to see the keywords on your page, and these keywords must be visible to your users. The easy approach is to either create content around your keyword, or naturally weave your keyword into the page. I'm not saying your page should look like the following example.

"Welcome to the NFL jersey store. Here we have NFL jerseys galore, with a wide range of NFL jerseys including women's NFL jerseys, men's NFL jerseys and children's NFL jerseys and much, much more."

This approach may have worked 10 years ago, but not now. The keyword should appear naturally in your page. Any attempts to go bonkers with your keywords will look horrible and may set off spam filters in search engines. Use your keyword naturally throughout the content. Repeating your keyword once or twice is more than enough.

It's really that simple.

Next up, you need to ensure you have a handful of LSI keywords on your page. LSI stands for Latent Semantic Indexing. Don't be discouraged by the technical term, LSI keywords is an SEO term for related phrases. Google believes a page is more naturally written and has a higher tendency to be good quality and relevant, if it also includes relevant and related keywords to your main phrase.

To successfully optimize a page, you need to have your main keywords and related keywords in the page. Find two or three related keywords to your main keyword and repeat these in the page once or two times each. LSIGraph is a great tool for finding keywords Google considers related to your main keywords. Use LSIGraph and your keyword research to determine a list of the most related keywords.

LSIGraph– Free
https://lsigraph.com/

Areas you can weave keywords into the page include:
- Meta description and meta title tags
- Navigation anchor text
- Navigation anchor title tags
- Headings (h1, h2, h3, and h4 tags)
- Content text
- Bolded and italicized text
- Internal links in content
- Image filename, image alt tag and image title tag
- Video filename, video title

HOW TO GET MORE PEOPLE CLICKING ON YOUR RANKINGS IN GOOGLE.

Meta tags have been widely misunderstood as mysterious pieces of code SEO professionals mess around with, and the secret to attaining top rankings. This couldn't be further from the truth.

The function of meta tags is really quite simple. Meta tags are bits of code on your site controlling how your site appears in Google.

If you don't fill out your meta tags, Google will automatically use text from your site to create your search listing. This is exactly what you don't want Google to do, otherwise it can end up looking like gibberish! Fill out these tags correctly, and you can increase the number of people clicking to your site from the search engine results.

Below is an example of the meta tag code.

```
<title>Paul's NFL Jerseys</title>
<meta description="Buy NFL jerseys online. Wide range of colors and sizes." />
<meta name="robots" content="noodp, noydir"/>
```

Below is an example of how a page with the above meta tag should appear as a search engine result in Google:

Paul's NFL Jerseys
Buy Paul's NFL jerseys online. Wide range of colors and sizes. Free delivery and free returns. We accept international orders!
http://www.yoursite.com/

Pretty simple, huh?

The title tag has a character limit of roughly 70 characters in Google. Use any more than 70 characters and it is likely Google will truncate your title tag in the search engine results.

The meta description tag has a character limit of roughly 155 characters. Just like the title tag, Google will shorten your listing if it has any more than 155 characters in the tag.

The last meta robots tag indicates to Google you want to control how your listing appears in the search results. It's good to include this, while unlikely, it's possible Google can ignore your tags and instead use those listed on other directories such as the Open Directory Project and the Yahoo Directory.

To change these tags on your site you have three options:

1. Use the software your site is built on. Most content management systems have the option to change these tags. If it doesn't, you may need to install an SEO plugin to change these tags.

2. Speak with your web designer or web developer to manually change your Meta tags for you.

3. If you are a tech-savvy person and are familiar with HTML, you can change these tags in the code yourself.

SITE LOAD SPEED—GOOGLE MAGIC DUST.

How fast (or slow) your site loads is a strong factor Google considers when deciding how it should rank your pages in the search results.

Google's former head of web spam, Matt Cutts, publicly admitted fast load speed is a positive ranking factor.

If your site is as slow as a dead snail, then it is likely your site is not living up to its potential in the search engines. If your site load time is average, improving the load speed is an opportunity for an easy SEO boost.

Not only is load speed a contributing factor to achieving top rankings in Google, extensive industry reports have shown for each second shaved off a site, there is an average increase of 7% to the site conversion rate. In other words, the faster your site loads, the more chance you have of people completing a sale or filling out an enquiry form. Load speed is not an aspect of your site to be overlooked.

Every site is built differently, with an endless variation of server configurations, which means improving your load speed isn't as simple as following a checklist. However, the following techniques are common improvements that will work on most sites.

Common load speed improvements.

- Host your site in the city where your customers reside and load speeds will increase.
- Alternatively, use a CDN (content delivery network) to host your site on servers all over the world. Visitors will get super-fast load speeds regardless of location. Popular CDN services include Amazon CloudFront, MaxCDN and Cloudfare.
- Enable load speed technologies like caching, compression, minification and HTTP/2. Most platforms have plugins for this, e.g. W3 Total Cache is a popular plugin offering most of these features on WordPress.
- Find large files on your site and shrink them. Use software like Adobe Photoshop and you can compress image file sizes from 3MB down to 250KB without visual loss in quality, by using Photoshop's "save for web" feature. An easy-win for image-heavy sites.

The above are just a handful of the infinite possibilities for improving a site's load speed. Fortunately, there's several tools making easy to identify speed improvements, and speed bottlenecks, irrespective of the technology your site is built on.

Load speed analysis tools.

1. Google Page Speed Insights
https://developers.google.com/speed/pagespeed/insights

Google's great free tool, Page Speed Insights, will give you a page load score out of 100. You can see how well your load speed compares to other sites. You can also see how well your site loads on mobile and desktop. Scores closer to 100 are near perfect.

After running a test on your site, the tool will give you a list of high priority, medium priority and low priority areas for improvement. You can forward these on to your developer to speed up your site, or if you are a bit of a tech-head, you can have a crack at fixing these up yourself.

2. Test My Site - Think With Google
https://www.thinkwithgoogle.com/feature/testmysite/

Around late June, 2017 Google updated their mobile load speed testing tool, Test My Site, to include benchmarking reports against industry competitors. This tool is both easy-to-use and indispensable for finding easy-win load speed improvements for mobile users — and handy for seeing how your website performs against competitors.

You might be shocked the first time you use this tool — many site owners discover they are losing up to 30%-50% of traffic, due to poor loading time on 3G mobile devices, not a great outlook.

Fortunately, the handy tool provides free reports and actionable recommendations on how to supercharge your load speed with a strong focus on improvements for mobile users. If you follow the recommendations and get your site performing better than competitors, you can make out like a bandit in the search results, with load speed being a top ranking factor driving the search results.

3. Pingdom Tools – Website Speed Test
https://tools.pingdom.com/
Pingdom Tools Website Speed Test is the cream of the crop when it comes to load speed tools, providing detailed breakdowns of files and resources slowing your site down, listing file-sizes of individual files, server load times, and much more. It goes into much greater depth than the other tools, though probably best suited for a web developer or someone with a basic level of experience building websites.

After the test is completed, if you scroll down you will see a list of files each visitor has to download each time they visit your site. Large images are easy targets for load speed improvements. If you have any images over 200kb, these can usually be compressed in Photoshop and shrunk down to a fraction of the size without any quality loss. Take a note of any large files, send them to your web developer or web designer, and ask them to compress the files to a smaller file size.

4. Lighthouse – Tools For Web Developers – Google
https://developers.google.com/web/tools/lighthouse/

For advanced developers working on complicated projects or sites — i.e. programmers who know what a Node module is — Google released a powerful Chrome extension called Lighthouse. Lighthouse provides reports on website performance, accessibility, adherence to programming best practices, SEO and more — with actionable steps on improving each of these areas. While owners of basic websites probably won't get additional insights from this tool, on top of recommendations provided by the earlier tools, programming ninjas looking for a well-rounded tool to enhance his or her performance chops will find Google's Lighthouse is the Swiss Army knife of site performance analysis.

THE USUAL SUSPECTS—SITEMAPS.XML AND ROBOTS.TXT.

Sitemaps.xml

Search engines automatically look for a special file on each site called the sitemaps.xml file. Having this file on your site is a must for making it easy for search engines to discover pages on your site. Sitemaps are essentially a giant map of all of the pages on your site. Fortunately, creating this file and getting it on to your site is a straightforward process.

Most CMS systems have a sitemap file automatically generated. This includes systems like Wordpress, Magento, Shopify. If this is not the case on your site, you may need to install a plugin or use the free XML Sitemaps Generator tool. The XML Sitemaps Generator will automatically create a sitemaps.xml file for you.

XML Sitemaps Generator
https://www.xml-sitemaps.com/

Next ask your web developer or web designer to upload it into the main directory of your site or do it yourself if you have FTP access. Once uploaded, the file should be publicly accessible with an address like the below example:

http://www.yoursite.com/sitemaps.xml

Once you have done this, you should submit your sitemap to the Google Search Console account for your site.

If you do not have a Google Search Console account, the below article by Google gives simple instructions for web developers or web designers to set this up.

Add a website property – Search Console Help
https://support.google.com/webmasters/answer/34592

Login to your account and click on your site. Under "site configuration" click "sitemaps" and submit your sitemap.

Robots.txt

Another must-have for every site is a robots.txt file. This should sit in the same place as your sitemaps.xml file. The address to this file should look the same as the example below:

http://www.yoursite.com/robots.txt

The robots.txt file is a simple file that exists so you can tell the areas of your site you *don't* want Google to list in the search engine results.

There is no real boost from having a robots.txt file on your site. It is essential you check to ensure you don't have a robots.txt file blocking areas of your site you want search engines to find.

The robots.txt file is just a plain text document, its contents should look something like below:

robots.txt good example

User-agent: *
Disallow: /admin
User-agent: *
Disallow: /logs

If you want your site to tell search engines to not crawl your site, it should look like the next example. If you *do not* want your entire site blocked, you must make sure it does *not* look like the example below. It is always a good idea to double check it is not set up this way, just to be safe.

robots.txt - blocking the entire site

User-agent: *
Disallow: /

The forward slash in this example tells search engines their software should not visit the home directory.

To create your robots.txt file, simply create a plain text document with Notepad if you are on Windows, or Textedit if you are on Mac OS. Make sure the file is saved as a plain text document, and use the "robots.txt good example" as an indication on how it should look. Take care to list any directories you do not want search engines to visit, such as internal folders for staff, admin areas, CMS back-end areas, and so on.

If there aren't any areas you would like to block, you can skip your robots.txt file altogether, but just double check you don't have one blocking important areas of the site like the above example.

DUPLICATE CONTENT—CANONICAL TAGS AND OTHER FUN.

In later chapters I will describe how Google Panda penalizes sites with duplicate content. Unfortunately, many site content management systems will sometimes automatically create multiple versions of one page.

For example, let's say your site has a product page on socket wrenches, but because of the system your site is built on, the exact same page can be accessed from multiple URLs from different areas of your site:

http://www.yoursite.com/products.aspx?=23213
http://www.yoursite.com/socket-wrenches
http://www.yoursite.com/tool-kits/socket-wrenches

In the search engine's eyes this is confusing as hell and multiple versions of the page are considered duplicate content.

To account for this, you should always ensure a special tag is placed on every page in your site, called the canonical tag.

The canonical tag indicates the original version of a web page to search engines. By telling Google the page you consider to be the "true" version of the page into the tag, you can indicate which page you want listed in the search results.

Choose the URL that is the most straightforward for users, this should usually be the URL that reads like plain English.

Using the earlier socket wrenches example, by using the tag below, Google would be more likely to display the best version of the page in the search engine results.

```
<link rel="canonical
" href="http://www.yoursite.com/socket-wrenches
"/>
```

As a general rule, include this tag on every page on your site, shortly before the </head> tag in the code.

USABILITY—THE NEW SEO EXPLAINED.

Mobiles and tablets have overtaken desktops in the vicious battle for Internet market share, making up 56% of all traffic in 2017. To keep a good experience for all users, Google are increasingly giving advantages to sites providing a good experience for users on all devices. Usability has increased importance in the SEO industry as a result, as many SEO pundits found you can get an advantage simply by making your site easy to use.

For example, let's say a mobile user is searching for late night pizza delivery in Los Angeles. One local business has a site with a large amount of backlinks but no special support for mobile users, it's difficult for the user to navigate because it doesn't automatically fit to the screen, and the menu text is small and hard to use on a touch screen.

Another competing local business has low amounts of backlinks, but good support for mobile users. Its design fits perfectly to the screen and has special navigation designed for mobile users, making it easy to use.

In many cases, the second site will now rank higher than the first, for mobile users. This is just one example of how usability can have a significant impact on your rankings.

While a term like usability can understandably seem a little vague, let's look at practical steps to improve your usability and the SEO strength of your site.

1. Make your site accessible for all devices.

Make your site accessible and easy for all users: desktop, mobile and tablet. The simple way to do this is to make sure your site is responsive, which means it automatically resizes across all devices and has mobile-friendly navigation for mobile users. Mobile support is covered in more detail, in the Mobile SEO Update section in the Google's Algorithm Updates chapter later in this book, but you can enter your site into the tool below quickly to see if Google registers your site as mobile friendly.

Mobile friendly Test - Google
https://search.google.com/test/mobile-friendly

2. Increase your content quality.

Gone are the days of hiring a bunch of writers in India to bulk out the content on your site. It needs to be proofread and edited, and the more "sticky" you make your content, the better results you will get. If you provide compelling content, users will spend more time on your site and are less likely to bounce back to the search results. Users will also be much more likely to share your content. Google will see this and give your rankings a boost.

3. Use clean code in your site.

There's a surprisingly high amount of sites with dodgy code, difficult for both search engines and Internet browsers to read. If there are HTML code errors in your site, which means, if it hasn't been coded according to industry best practices, it's possible your design will break when your site is viewed on different browsers, or even worse, confuse search engines when they come along and look at your site. Run your site through the below tool and ask your web developer to fix any errors.

Web standards validator
https://validator.w3.org/

4. Take it easy on the popups and advertisements.

Sites with spammy and aggressive ads are often ranked poorly in the search results. The SEO gurus have reached no consensus on the amount of ads leading to a penalty from Google, so use your common sense. Ensure advertisements don't overshadow your content and occupy the majority of screen real estate.

5. Improve the overall "operability" of your site.

Does your site have slow web hosting, or a bunch of broken links and images? Simple technical oversights like these contribute to a poor user experience.

Make sure your site is with a reliable web hosting company and doesn't go down in peak traffic. Even better, make sure your site is hosted on a server in your local city, and this will make it faster for local users.

Next up, chase up any 404-errors with your web developer. 404 errors are errors indicating users are clicking on links in your site and being sent to an empty page. It contributes to a poor user experience in Google's eyes. Fortunately, these errors are easy fixed.

You can find 404 errors on your site by logging into your Google Search Console account, clicking on your site, then clicking on "Crawl" and "Crawl Errors." Here you will find a list of 404 errors. If you click on the error and then click "Linked From" you can find the pages with the broken links. Fix these yourself, or discuss with your web developer.

Google Search Console
https://search.google.com/search-console/about

If you want external tools to speed up improving your site's usability, I have found these two resources helpful:

BrowserStack - Free to try, plans start at $29 per month.
https://www.browserstack.com

BrowserStack allows you to test your site on over +700 different browsers at once. You can preview how your site works on tablets, mobile devices, and all the different browsers such as Chrome, Firefox, Safari, Internet Explorer, and so on. It's helpful for making sure it displays correctly across many different devices.

Try My UI - Free to try, additional test results start at $35. https://www.trymyui.com/

Try My UI provides videos, audio narration, surveys of users going through your site, and reports on any difficulties they uncover. Usability tests are good for larger projects requiring objective feedback from normal users. The first test result is free, making Try My UI a good usability test provider to start with.

MOBILE SUPPORT—IMPORTANT SEO EXPLAINED IN SIMPLE TERMS.

On April, 2015, Google released a game changing update for the SEO industry. Sites with solid mobile support started ranking higher in the Google mobile search results. Sites with no mobile support generally started ranking lower in mobile search results.

Whether we like it or not, mobile users are here to stay and Google are driving the mobile revolution. With the largest mobile app store in the world, the largest mobile operating system in the world, and the largest amount of mobile search users, it's safe to say mobile users are a priority for Google.

If you are not supporting mobile users, it's important to implement mobile support, not just for better search engine results, but for better sales and conversions — quite simply, the majority of your traffic is coming from mobile users.

How to best support mobile users.

If you want to increase support for mobile devices and be more search engine friendly, you have three options:

1. Create a responsive site.

Responsive sites are the cream of the crop when it comes to sites that support both desktop and mobile devices. With responsive sites, both mobile and desktop users see the same pages and same content, and everything is automatically sized to fit the screen. It's also becoming more common for WordPress templates and new sites to feature a responsive layout.

2. Dynamically serve different content to mobile and desktop users.

You can ask your web developer to detect which devices are accessing your site and automatically deliver a different version of your site catered to the device. This is a complicated setup, better suited for large sites with thousands of pages, with complicated infrastructure, when a responsive approach is not possible.

3. Host your mobile content on a separate subdomain, e.g. m.yoursite.com

While Google stated they support this implementation, I recommend against it. You need a lot of redirects in place and must jump through giant hoops to ensure search engines recognize your special mobile subdomain as a copy of your main site. Responsive sites are popular for good reason: it's easier and cheaper to maintain one site rather than both maintaining a desktop copy of your site and maintaining a separate mobile copy of your site, on a mobile subdomain.

Improving performance in the mobile search results.

Google stated mobile support is straightforward, either your site supports mobile devices or it doesn't... Well it's not straightforward. You can get an edge over competitors by using a handful of tools to improve your mobile usability and make your site faster for mobile users. Run your site through Google's Mobile Friendly Test Tool to confirm if you support mobile users, use Google's "Test Your Mobile Speed and Performance" tool for actionable steps to speed up your mobile site, and review the Mobile Usability report in Google Search Console and check for any errors worth fixing — and if you're lazy like me, delegate. Send the reports and errors over to your web developer and get them fixed. Who doesn't like a competitive advantage? Work through these tools, make your mobile support better than competitors, and you will crush it in the search results.

Mobile Friendly Test Tool
https://search.google.com/test/mobile-friendly

Test Your Mobile Speed and Performance – Think With Google
https://www.thinkwithgoogle.com/feature/testmysite/

Mobile Usability – Google Search Console
https://www.google.com/webmasters/tools/mobile-usability

The technical details of building a responsive site are beyond the scope of this book and could fill an entire book. In fact, it does, I counted close to 17 responsive web design books on Amazon as I wrote this paragraph... That said, mobile SEO can be ridiculously simple.

If you have a responsive site that delivers the same content to mobile and desktop users, automatically resizes content to the screen, is fast and is user-friendly, all you have to do is follow the SEO recommendations in this book, and your mobile results will be top notch from an SEO perspective. Alternatively, follow one of the recommended implementations discussed earlier in this section.

For guidelines, direct from the horse's mouth so to speak, you can read Google's mobile support documentation for webmasters and web developers.

Mobile Friendly Sites – Google Developers
https://developers.google.com/search/mobile-sites/

GOOGLE'S SEARCH QUALITY GUIDELINES — AND HOW TO USE THEM TO YOUR ADVANTAGE.

Search quality is an increasingly popular topic in the blogosphere because it can have a massive impact on rankings. Why is this so? Making sure users are sent to high-quality and trustworthy search results is critical for Google to safeguard their position as providing the best all-round search experience.

While this sounds a little vague, you can use Google's search quality to your advantage and get an edge over competitors. Did you know that Google publicly published their "Search Quality Evaluator Guidelines", updated on July 27th, 2017? If you didn't, well now you do.

The document's 160-pages long, so presuming you don't consider a dense whitepaper leisurely reading, I'll list out the most important and actionable takeaways, so you can use them to your advantage.

Google Search Quality Evaluator Guidelines - Most Important Factors

In Google's whitepaper, they list out their holy-trio of most important factors when it comes to search quality. And here it is…

EAT... That's right, EAT... Expertise, Authority and Trust (EAT). Acronym choice aside, to establish quality, Google are looking at the expertise, authority and trustworthiness of the page and site. This includes things like the content quality and how aggressive ads are on your site. The reputation of the site and its authors, publicly-listed information about the site ownership, contact details, and several other factors.

Now we know what's important from a top-level perspective, let's zoom into actionable and practical takeaways straight out of the document that will affect the average Joe trying to nudge his way up the search results.

Search Quality Evaluator Guidelines — Key Takeaways

1. Real name, company name, and contact information listed on an about page. If you don't have this information listed on your website, why should Google, or anyone else for that matter, trust you? Better make sure you include it.

2. Excessive and unnatural internal structural links across sidebars and footers. If you've got 150-links in your footer, it's obvious to Google you're trying to do something sneaky, so be conservative with the footer and sidebar links. Keep it restricted to the most important pages on your site or what's useful for your users.

3. Over monetization of content. Specifically, if you are disguising advertisements as main content, or your advertisements occupy more real-estate than the main content, than one of Google's search evaluators will probably flag your site as spam. Take a common-sense approach with your ads, don't overdo it!

4. List editors & contributors. Are you publishing a bunch of articles under pseudonyms or generic usernames? Listing editors and contributors, i.e. real people, is more trustworthy and will increase the perceived quality of your page.

5. Provide sources. Publishing generic articles en masse without any reputable sources? You'll get a better-quality assessment, and a higher ranking, if you list sources for your articles. Listing sources shows the writer has performed diligence in their research and increases the credibility of the page.

6. Financial transaction pages. All you drop-shippers and ecommerce retailers out there stand up and take note — pages associated with financial transactions (shopping cart, checkout, product pages, etc.) must link to policy pages for refunds, returns, delivery information, and the terms and conditions of your site. Think about it from the user's perspective, if you are average Joe shopper thinking about buying something and the page doesn't list any of this information, how safe would you feel checking out?

7. Pages offering financial information must be of the highest quality. Google are stricter with these types of pages, as it falls into their "Your Money or Your Life" category — meaning it could affect the financial well-being of the user. If you're publishing this kind of content, make sure you're doing everything you can to provide high-quality, detailed articles, citing sources, fully disclosing financial relationships, and making it clear what author or company is behind the content.

That sums up the most important takeaways from the Google Search Evaluator Guidelines. If you haven't got them in your site, work 'em in and you'll get a leg up over your competitors, or worse, your rankings could suffer. And if you really, really want to sit down and read through the 160-page whitepaper on page-quality assessment, here it is for your enjoyment.

Search Quality Evaluator Guidelines – May, 2019
https://static.googleusercontent.com/media/guidelines.r aterhub.com/en//searchqualityevaluatorguidelines.pdf

READABILITY — SEO FOR THE FUTURE.

One of the strongest ranking factors has been flying under the radar, overlooked by many SEO professionals in their optimization checklists, leaving a golden opportunity for those that know about it. I'm talking about readability.

Google have been outspoken about readability as an important consideration for webmasters. Google's former head of web spam, Matt Cutts, publicly stated that poorly researched and misspelled content will rank poorly, and clarity should be your focus. And by readability, this means not just avoiding spelling mistakes, but making your content readable for the widest possible audience, with simple language and sentence structures.

Flesch readability has since surfaced in the Searchmetrics Google ranking factors report, showing a high correlation between high ranking sites and easy to read content. The Searchmetrics rankings report discovered sites appearing in the top 10 showed an average Flesch reading score of 76.00 — content that is fairly easy to read for 13-15 year old students and up.

It makes sense readability is a concern for Google. By encouraging search results to have content readable to a wide audience, Google maximise their advertising revenues. If Google were to encourage complicated results that mostly appeal to a smaller demographic, such as postgraduates, it would lower Google's general appeal and their market share.

You can achieve an on-page SEO boost, while also increasing your user engagement, by making your content readable to a wide audience. Run your content through a Flesch readability test. It will look at your word and sentence usage, and give you a score on how readable it is. Scores between 90-100 are easily understood by an 11 year old student, 60-70 easily understood by 13 to 15 year old students, and 0-30 best understood by University graduates. You can use the free tool below, and should aim for a readability score between 60-100. To improve your score, edit your content to use fewer words per sentence, and use words with a smaller number of syllables.

Readability Score
https://readable.com/

HOW TO ACCELERATE TRAFFIC AND RANKINGS WITH CONTENT MARKETING.

One of the most powerful on-page SEO strategies is adding more unique, fresh content to your site. If you consistently add new pages to your site, you are going to receive more traffic. In fact, not only can you increase your traffic, you can receive an *exponential* traffic increase as you publish more content.

It's a no-brainer when you think about it. This is why blogs, publishing and news-type sites consistently get good results in search engines. More content means more rankings, more visitors, and more sales. Let's look at getting started with improving your traffic by adding fresh content.

1. Post new content on a regular schedule.

If you are going to add new content to your site, you need to decide on a schedule and stick to it. This might seem obvious, but you would be surprised at the large number of businesses that talk about starting a blog and never get around to it. It's the businesses with a regular roster of adding content to their site that see regular increases in search rankings, increases in overall search engine performance, and a growing loyal audience. Without a dedicated roster or schedule, it will never get done.

If you don't have the capacity to create content yourself, or a budget to hire a full-time marketing assistant to create content, try hiring a ghostwriter.

Good quality writers can be sourced between $25-$75 USD per article and you can regularly churn out fresh content to your heart's content. Popular services can put you in touch with talented writers, such as Textbroker or the Problogger job board.

Textbroker
https://www.textbroker.com

Problogger Job Board
https://problogger.com/jobs/

2. Leverage your social media accounts.

It almost goes without saying, but you should be leveraging social media to drive traffic to new posts or pages added to your site.

Whenever you post new content, post it across all of your social media accounts. Then post it again in a couple of days and you will expose your content to a different segment of fans. You'll increase your social activity and as a result get higher rankings.

3. Link up your site to blog aggregators.

Blog directories are an easy opportunity for high-quality backlinks, available for anyone running a blog. A handful of large authority blog directories accept site submissions and syndicate content—an opportunity to build up referral traffic. Simply ensure you have a base level of content to start, and then submit your site. A link to your blog can be approved within a week or two.

Here's a handful of high-quality blog directories accepting submissions:

https://www.alltop.com/
https://www.blogarama.com/
https://blogs.botw.org/
https://www.eatonweb.com/

USER BEHAVIOR OPTIMIZATION—HOW TO USE GOOGLE'S MACHINE LEARNING TECHNOLOGY TO YOUR ADVANTAGE.

Ever heard of Project Pigeon, the top-secret World War 2 U.S. military project developing missiles guided by pigeons tapping on transparent screens?

Project Pigeon was developed by famous Harvard behavioral psychologist B. F. Skinner in the 1940s, later decommissioned, because in Skinner's words, "no one would take us seriously." Later, Skinner's more notable work on behavioral analysis was taken seriously, establishing behavioral psychology as a legitimate field of psychology.

How we behave online—tapping on screens—has become a hot focus point for Google, with user behavior signals, such as bounce rate, time-on-site, and click-through-rate, positioned strongly in Google's top 10 ranking factors. Google's machine learning algorithm RankBrain observes these behavior signals, recalculating search results in real-time. Fortunately, you can use this to your advantage and get higher rankings with user behavior optimization.

Improving user behavior on your site is no longer a 'nice-to-have'… It's a serious requirement for any SEO practitioner and powerful technique for anyone who wants to rank in the top-10 results.

Read on for actionable techniques for leveraging Google's machine learning algorithm to shoot your pages the top of the rankings faster than a pigeon guided missile.

Boosting Click-Through Rates.

Your click-through-rate (CTR) is the percentage of people who see your search listing and click on it. If more people click on your search result than others, this tells Google your page is appealing to users. Get higher-click-through-rates with these 7 techniques.

1. Fill out meta title and meta description tags on your target pages. Unfilled meta tags lead to automatically generated snippets by Google, which generally receive low CTRs. For every page on your site with unfilled meta tags, an SEO technician silently weeps.

2. Make meta tags compelling. Think actionable, descriptive and specific. Sell your page and make it clear why the user should click on your result instead of competing pages.

3. Use numbers and special characters to stand out. Specific numbers naturally attract higher click through rates. And special characters such as pipes, em-dashes and brackets make your rankings more eye catching, gaining more clicks.

4. Use keywords in URLs. URLs with keywords indicate your page is relevant at a quick glance, getting automatic clicks.

5. Use short URLs. Both users and Google like short URLs, and so do I. Case closed.

6. Target featured snippets and rich snippets. Rich results can gain up to 30% more clicks. The rich snippets chapter later in this book details targeting these types of rankings.

7. Improve low performing pages. Look through your Google Search Console keyword report for keywords with low CTRs. Improve the meta tags and URLs on those pages and make them more click worthy.

Which of the following examples do you think gets high click-through-rates and ranks higher in the search results?..

How to Save Money: 20 Simple Tips | DaveRamsey.com
https://www.daveramsey.com/blog/the-secret-to-saving-money

U.S. Bank BrandVoice: 8 Dos and Dont's For Saving Money In ...
https://www.forbes.com/sites/usbank/2019/11/01/8-dos-and-donts-f...

Boosting Time On Site.

Time-on-site, bounce-rates, pages-per-visit... These metrics measure similar things — are users sticking to your content like glue, or are they immediately clicking the back button to find a better result?

How users engage with your content is considered super important by Google's machine learning algo RankBrain, if you can improve your time-on-site, you can improve your rankings. Let's look at 4 simple techniques for getting users hooked to your content.

1. Increase internal links in your content. Creating relevant internal links within your content encourages users to open up more tabs and browse more pages on your site, 2 to 3 internal links per blog post is enough without becoming annoying.

2. Make your content readable. Use large font sizes, preferably 16px-18px so people don't need to fetch the magnifying glass to read your content. Use short and simple words. And break your content down into subheadings, numbered lists, short paragraphs and sentences.

3. Use longer word counts. It stands to reason it takes longer for users to read long articles. And according to study by Ahrefs, content with longer word counts naturally attract more links. Nice.

4. Use videos. Video will be 80% of all Internet traffic by 2021 according to a study by Cisco. Simply put, Internet users love video. Every user that watches a video on your page boosts your time-on-site metric in heavenly ways.

5. Use interactive media. Interactive media such as slideshows and online tools are time-tested techniques to boost your time-on-site and user engagement.

~

That sums it up for the on-page SEO chapter.

If you have a small business, the technical factors mentioned earlier in this chapter are what will make the difference — such as ensuring your site has the right keywords and is accessible for all users.

If you are doing SEO for a large company and need a large amount of traffic, regularly publishing new content and ensuring structural areas of your site are setup correctly are what will make the difference — such as regularly posting new blog posts, ensuring you have sitemaps working correctly, and no duplicate content or 404 errors.

What's most important is you act. On-page SEO is often the easiest part of SEO. The power is in your hands to fix these areas in your site. Remember small changes can lead to big results. Put these methods to practice and start improving your rankings.

Just like the keyword research steps, for readers who want to put the theory into practice, all on-page optimization tips from this chapter are included in the SEO checklist. I recommend finishing the book before downloading the checklist and the on-page SEO steps, so you are familiar with the theory behind the practical steps.

LINK BUILDING. HOW TO RANK EXTREMELY HIGH ON GOOGLE.

WHY IS LINK BUILDING SO IMPORTANT?

The previous chapter described how to make your site visible to search engines and how to optimize keywords by using on-page SEO. If you want to see your rankings improve by leaps and bounds, then your site needs links.

You may have wondered what makes link building so important, especially when there are so many factors Google use to rank sites.

The truth is, links are such a strong factor, it is unlikely you will rank high for a keyword if you are competing against sites with more backlinks.

When you think about it, links are the currency of the web. Each time a page links to another, it is a vote for the value of the page being linked to. If a page provides massive value to Internet users, it stands to reason it will be linked to from other sites. This is why links are such a strong factor in Google's algorithm.

Link building is the key to ranking your site high in the search engine results.

THE DIRTY LITTLE SECRET NO ONE WANTS TO TELL YOU ABOUT LINK BUILDING.

There are a lot of opinions circulating the Internet about the best kind of links to build to your site. So much so, they often escalate into heated discussions.

What is the best link? A link from a government site or from a high trafficked blog? Is it better to get a link from a highly relevant site or from a site with a lot of social media activity?

The dirty secret no-one wants to tell you about link building is *there is no single best kind of link*.

If this weren't the case, Google wouldn't work. Everyone would go out and find a way to spam their way to the top of the rankings very quickly. Having thousands of one type of link pointing to a page is suspicious and a clear sign the site owner is gaming the system.

That said, as a rule, you should try to build links on authoritative, relevant and high-quality sites. High-quality, relevant links are much stronger than links from low-quality, unrelated sites.

HOW TO ACQUIRE LINKS AND WHAT TO AVOID IN LINK BUILDING.

There are many stories floating around about business owners being slammed by Google for no good reason. Don't let the horror stories mislead you.

In most cases, what really happened is the webmaster was doing something clearly suspicious or outdated, like building thousands of links to their site from link directories, and then their rankings suddenly dropped off from Google's top 10 search results.

If you don't exhibit overly spammy behavior in your link building, as a general rule you will be OK.

These best practices will ensure you acquire links correctly and don't break Google's terms of service:

1. Acquire links naturally and evenly over time. Your links should be attained consistently and organically.

In fact, Google has made its approach with assessing link acquisition in relation to time public knowledge. Patent US20050071741 outlines how Google analyzes the age of links and the rate they are acquired and then uses this information to calculate the search results.

If you don't fancy reading up on patents in your spare time, then just remember to gradually build up your links over time, so Google sees that your website is acquiring links organically. Don't go out and buy one thousand links pointing to your site overnight or you're sure to set off a red flag in Google's system and get into its bad books.

2. As a rule, don't purchase links. Buying links with the intention of boosting your rankings is against Google's terms of service and you risk being penalized. These kinds of links may work, but are generally not worth the potential damage, unless you are confident you know what you are doing.

3. Forget about link-swapping or link-trading schemes. These are completely obvious to Google, and either no longer work or may harm your site. This goes against common knowledge, but I've achieved countless number one rankings for ridiculously competitive keywords without ever swapping links. Link-swapping is extremely time-consuming and completely unnecessary. Get by without it.

4. Don't spam message boards, article sites or blog comments with crappy content. This might work temporarily, but strategies such as these are outdated very quickly.

5. There are paid networks out there offering to build new links to your site for a low monthly fee each month. Never use them. These networks are against Google's terms of service and using them is a quick way to ensure you find yourself in hot water with Google.

ANCHOR TEXT. WHAT'S ALL THE FUSS?

There has been some controversy around anchor text, as touched on in a previous chapter. Anchor text is the text contained in a link. Anchor text *was* one of the strongest factors for achieving top rankings.

If you had one thousand links to your site with "NFL football jerseys" as the link text, and competitors only had a handful of links with the same anchor text, it was likely you would rank number one. That is, until Google's Penguin update effectively put an end for SEOs using "exact match" anchor text as their strategy. Now it is just simply too risky.

Not only is it no longer as effective as it once was, building hundreds of "exact match" links to a site actually can prevent it from ranking for that keyword.

So then, you might wonder, what is the best way to build up anchor text?

It should be natural.

It is OK to have your targeted keyword in your anchor text, but it should not be the only keyword or the main keyword in all of your links, and there should be a mix of related keywords.

If you think about it, this is a pattern all legitimate sites naturally attract. It defies logic that a quality site would automatically be linked with the exact same text throughout the entire World Wide Web.

Look over the below examples to see a bad anchor text profile compared to a natural anchor text profile:

Bad anchor text – external links
http://www.examplefootballbrand.com/football-jerseys.html
NFL football jerseys - 200 links

Good anchor text
http://www.examplefootballbrand.com/football-jerseys.html
examplefootballbrand - 50 links
NFL football jersey store - 10 links
NFL football jerseys - 5 links
http://www.example.com - 25 links
football jersey store - 5 links
football jerseys online - 5 links
football jacket store - 15 links
click here - 7 links
website - 15 links

The above good anchor text example illustrates the natural way sites accumulate links over time. Your target keyword should not be the most linked phrase to the page.

You can learn a lot by looking at the search engine results ranking in Google, enter high-ranking sites into Link Explorer, and looking at their anchor text. You'll notice almost every top-ranking page has natural anchor text, like the good example above.

Track your link-building efforts and keep them in a spreadsheet. This way you can monitor your anchor text and make sure it fits in with best practices.

Link Explorer
https://moz.com/link-explorer

SIMPLE TO ADVANCED LINK BUILDING STRATEGIES.

The link building strategies below will help you build up quality links pointing to your site, and give Google a nudge to rank your site higher, ranging from simple tactics for the small business, right up to the enterprise-level SEO agency looking to roll out links on a large scale.

Directory links.

Directory links are a tried and true form of link building that received some flack in recent years. This is due to Google penalizing spammers who built ridiculous amounts of low-quality directory links to their site.

Directory links shouldn't be overlooked. In fact, directory links should be the first place to start with any link building project. There's a solid amount of high-quality business directories where you can get powerful and strong backlinks built with a minimum of effort.

But just to be safe, your directory links should not make up much more than 10-20% of your total links. They must also be relevant and quality sites, i.e. not sites with web addresses like seolinksdirectory.com or freelinksdirectory.com. Sites like these just smell of spam! Before building a link on a directory, ask yourself, "Does this look like a legitimate and trustworthy website?" If the answer is no, then move on and focus on legitimate, quality sites only.

To find relevant directories, use the below search terms in Google, replacing "keyword" with your targeted keyword or industry, and you can find relevant directories for your niche:

keyword + submit
keyword + add url
keyword + add link
keyword + directory
keyword + resources

Here is a short list of business directories to get you started:

https://www.linkedin.com/
https://www.bingplaces.com/
http://www.yelp.com/
https://www.mapquest.com/
https://www.yellowpages.com/
https://www.manta.com/
https://www.local.com/
https://www.citysearch.com/
https://www.merchantcircle.com/

Stealing competitor's links.

Stealing competitor's links is an old-school tactic receiving a resurgence in recent times, due to Google's increased focus on links from quality sites, making it more difficult to find easy link opportunities.

If your competitor has done all the heavy lifting, why not take advantage of their hard work. Use the below sites to export your competitors' backlinks. By looking through their links you can often find link opportunities to build links pointing to your site. In most cases, you can be confident you are going after SEO-friendly link sources if the competitor is already ranking well in Google.

Ahrefs Backlink Checker – Free to try, then $99 per month.
https://www.ahrefs.com/

Majestic SEO Backlink Checker – Free to try, then $49 per month.
https://majestic.com

Link Explorer – Free to try, then $179 per month
https://moz.com/link-explorer

Video link building.

Google loves videos, and it especially loves videos from video powerhouse YouTube. Probably because Google owns YouTube… If you want the opportunity to capture visitors from the world's largest video search engine, posting videos will considerably help your SEO.

Post relevant how-to guides, industry news updates and instructional videos for the best response from users. Then link to the relevant pages on your site in the description.

The key to success in video link building is to ensure the video and your description are related. You should aim to have your targeted keyword or relevant keywords on the page somewhere.

And don't worry. Your video doesn't have to be on par with the latest Martin Scorsese masterpiece. It can be a simple 5 or 10-minute video, educating visitors with useful knowledge about your topic. Just focus on making it contribute value for the viewer.

The tools below can help with quickly creating videos and uploading them to the web.

OBS Studio
https://obsproject.com/
OBS Studio is free, open source screen recording software allowing you to record high-quality screencasts from your own computer. You can download video files in high quality after you have finished or even make live streams. OBS Studio is free, works on Windows, Mac and Linux, but can be a little technical to use. User friendly alternatives include QuickTime Player's native screen recording function for Mac users, or a paid screen recording app like Camtasia.

High-quality sites you can easily visit, upload videos and get backlinks from:

https://www.youtube.com/
https://www.veoh.com/
https://www.dailymotion.com/
https://www.metacafe.com/
https://www.archive.org/

Link bait.

Link bait is a new and effective strategy for building high-quality and powerful links on a large scale. Link bait is great because you create content once, but you can have thousands of people over the Internet sharing and linking to your content, while you sit back and put your feet up.

But what is link bait exactly? Link bait is any kind of compelling content that naturally acquires links from other sites as a result.

While there is an art to creating link bait successfully, you would be surprised how easy it is to earn links and social media activity with this strategy. The key is, your content must be so valuable it would almost be worth paying for.

To create this content, you should use your expertise or even hire researchers to put together juicy industry content that lends itself to being shared. If there are already 10 blog posts or whitepapers on the same topic, then you're doing it wrong. Try and make it original, substantial and useful.

Wrap up this content into a whitepaper, top 10 list, an easy to understand infographic, or a downloadable resource and make it compelling enough for visitors to read and share.

Promote this content heavily through your site and social media accounts. Encourage readers to share the post at the bottom of the content. Make sharing the content as easy as possible and you will maximize results.

Next up, find popular link bait in your industry or niche. Then use a link analysis tool such as Ahrefs or Link Explorer to pull a list of sites linking to the popular content. Send out a quick email blast to site owners and bloggers to let them know about your bigger and much better resource.

If you really want to take link baiting to the next level, write and publish a compelling press release about your link bait content. With a press release, it can be exposed to thousands of journalists and potentially has a chance of attracting media coverage.

You might be wondering what a successful link baiting campaign looks like. I've listed examples below:

WordPress SEO
https://yoast.com/wordpress-seo/
Joost de Valk is well known in the SEO industry, in some part due to his one page guide to WordPress SEO that is updated every month or so. This guide has earned many links and shares over many years.

101 Motivational Business Quotes
https://www.quicksprout.com/101-motivational-business-quotes/
Excellent example of a great link bait article that went viral, and could be outsourced for pennies on the dollar.

Types of link bait:
- Infographics
- How-to guides
- Beginner guides
- Breaking news
- Top 10 lists
- Industry reports
- Whitepapers

Pictochart -Free to start
https://www.piktochart.com/
Great service for infographic generation, has an easy drag and drop interface to put infographics together in minutes.

Prlog
https://www.prlog.org/
Prlog offers entry-level free press release syndication services, with additional coverage for an added fee.

PRNewswire
https://www.prnewswire.com/
Many PR firms will simply write a press release and then release it to PRNewswire and charge a premium for doing so. Cut out the middleman, write up your press release yourself, and you can get massive PR for a fraction of the cost of hiring a PR agent. Packages start at $425 USD and scale up for increased syndication.

Finding guest post opportunities.

Guest posting has become standard practice for many link builders, for its effectiveness in getting high-quality and highly-relevant and contextual links — the type of links Google loves.

Finding guest post opportunities is fairly straightforward. Simply do a few Google searches with the following search terms and you'll find some quality placements. This strategy does require that yourself or your writer produce articles with a reasonable standard of quality... Articles that are well-written, researched, articulated, and preferably citing sources, are more likely to get social shares and high user engagement — which will increase the strength of the links. Further, if you have a reasonable sized social platform behind you — the editor or site owner might be more enticed to post your blog post.

On the other hand, if you try this strategy on a large scale with cheap, poorly written outsourced articles with bad grammar, providing little benefit for users, it's possible you could harm your rankings. Quality is critical for a successful guest posting strategy.

Try the following search queries in Google, replacing "keyword" with your industry, niche or topic, for finding guest post opportunities. And use the Google Chrome extension, Link Clump, to copy and paste the search results into a spreadsheet, so you can reach out to the blogs for a guest post placement — which will be covered later in this chapter.

keyword "guest post by"
keyword "guest post"
keyword "guest article"
keyword "guest author"
keyword "contributor"
keyword "guest contributor"

Link Clump
https://tinyurl.com/link-clump-chrome

Broken link building.

Broken link building is a new, but effective strategy. With this new strategy, you can reach out to quality sites with broken links on their pages, and use this as an opportunity to convince the site administrator to provide an updated link to your site.

When you find a broken link, let them know the broken link exists and you have an alternative resource on your site that will benefit their readers. With this strategy, you should create a linkable resource on your site. This makes it very easy for the webmaster to point the link to your replacement.

Use the formulas below to find potential pages with broken links, replacing "keyword" with the keyword you are targeting:

keyword useful links
keyword useful resources
keyword useful sites

keyword recommended links
keyword recommended resources
keyword recommended sites
keyword suggested links
keyword suggested resources
keyword suggested sites
keyword more links
keyword more resources
keyword more sites
keyword related links
keyword related resources
keyword related sites

If you want to automate this process, the service below will do the heavy lifting, and give you a list of sites with broken links and contact details so you can quickly reach out to the webmaster.

Broken linkbuilding - $67 monthly
https://www.brokenlinkbuilding.com/
This tool is comprehensive, but comes at a price. By typing in keywords you are targeting, the broken link building tool will find a solid amount of broken link opportunities. Saves time and finds quality opportunities.

Broken brand mentions.

Broken brand mentions are a fast, simple and reliable form of link building you can use for almost every SEO project. It goes like this: in some cases, when someone mentions your brand they forget to post a link. Track mentions of your brand, and where suitable, reach out and ask for a link back to your site.

Use the below tools to track mentions of your brand. If you see a mention of your brand without a link, send a quick email to the author, and they will often be happy to link to your site.

Brand monitoring sites I've found useful:

Google Alerts - Free
https://www.google.com/alerts
Google Alerts is a very powerful brand monitoring tool. Get email alerts whenever your brand name is mentioned, or, when any keyword is mentioned across the web. Both free and powerful, making it worth checking out.

Mention - Free to try, pricing starts at $25 per month.
https://mention.com/en/
Mention is a powerful brand-monitoring tool that will send an email alert when your brand is mentioned online, so you can respond quickly.

Paid links.

Paid links are against Google's terms-of-service, these below link building tactics do work and can fly under the radar. Needless to say, if you're feeling daring, you've been warned and I take no responsibility for what happens as a result of paid link strategies.

Donate to charities & non-profits.

Charities and non-profits sites often have a donors' page. Search for "site:.org + donors" or "site:.org + sponsors" in Google for a list of organizations that have these pages, offer a donation, and request a listing on the page.

Better Business Bureau.

Links from the Better Business Bureau are among the best links you can receive. Better Business Bureau links will pass authority and trust. Check your listing to see if you are already linking back to your site, and if you're not already a member, then consider signing up.

LINK OUTREACH—SCALING UP HIGH QUALITY LINK BUILDING CAMPAIGNS.

Link outreach is a common and powerful link technique in use by SEO professionals these days, and for good reason—it's an effective way to scale up your high-quality and relevant links.

What to avoid with link outreach campaigns.

Before we jump into link outreach techniques, Google publicly stated guidelines on this practice and it's important to know what to avoid, so you don't get into Google's naughty book.

Here's a direct quote of the combination of factors Google consider bad-practice, as discussed in their guidelines published May 2017, about large-scale article campaigns:

- Stuffing keyword-rich links to your site in your articles.
- Having the articles published across many different sites; alternatively, having a large number of articles on a few large, different sites.
- Using or hiring article writers that aren't knowledgeable about the topics they're writing on.
- Using the same or similar content across these articles; alternatively, duplicating the full content of articles found on your own site (in which case use of rel='canonical' and rel='nofollow' is advised).

The guidelines are a little vague... The reason being, Google can't completely outlaw guest-posting, nor can they outlaw site owners talking with other site owners to collaborate — that would hardly be fair and an over-reach on Google's part.

Google are mostly concerned the articles are relevant, high-quality, posted on relevant sites, aren't stuffed with extreme numbers of links pointing to your site, and you're not annoying a billion site owners with spammy unpersonalized email blasts filling up their inboxes. Avoid these practices, and you'll avoid getting a slap by Mr. Google.

Here's the official guidelines from the guys over at Google HQ if you want to read up further.

A reminder about links in large-scale article campaigns - Google Webmaster Central Blog https://webmasters.googleblog.com/2017/05/a-reminder-about-links-in-large-scale.html

Steps for link outreach campaigns.

Typically, there are two steps for link outreach campaigns:

1. Prospecting - finding link opportunities and finding contact information.
2. Outreach - writing and sending emails, follow ups, replies and managing relationships.

We've already covered link opportunities, such as looking through competitor's backlinks and finding guest post opportunities, so let's jump into the nitty gritty of finding contact information and conducting a link outreach campaign.

Finding contact information.

Finding contact information is easy with the right tools. First, you can use a standalone tool for automatically finding contact details on sites while browsing through link opportunities, like Hunter.io's very handy Chrome extension which automatically finds contact details for you, or you can make things simple and try an all-in-one email outreach platform covered in the next section, that both finds contact details and sends emails.

Secondly, you should track all your link opportunities in a spreadsheet or Google Doc, and make sure you leave a personal note for each link opportunity, which will be later dynamically inserted into your email (more on this later).

Hunter
https://hunter.io/
Hunter is purely focused on finding contact details and very good at it. It has a nice Chrome plugin that shows you the contact details it can find for a particular site while browsing. Free plans include up to 100-contact information requests, for more contact requests plans start at $39 per month.

Personalization.

Whichever outreach platform you use, you should always ensure your email is personalized in some way. This includes addressing the author or editor by name, mentioning a recent article that captured your interest, a similarity between your websites, or how you have a particular resource or topic that aligns with something the site owner is passionate about. Leave a note of this in your spreadsheet while reviewing opportunities...

Remember, there's a big difference between contacting a site owner with a relevant, personalized email and a mutually-beneficial opportunity for collaboration, and a big spammy email blast to a thousand site owners with the same email template — which could quickly get you in hot water with Google. Don't skip the personalization.

Outreach platforms and scheduling emails.

There's a growing number of outreach platforms due to the increasing popularity of this technique. Here are some popular options on the market. Some only send emails, others offer end-to-end outreach campaign management, including finding prospects, contact details, sending emails, automated follow ups, the whole kit and caboodle. Anyways, here they are.

Mailshake
https://mailshake.com/
Mailshake is pure-outreach. You will need to provide contact information yourself. It is very effective at sending personalized email campaigns, and you can import personalization info including name, address and a personal message via a csv file. Includes automatic follow-ups, email template libraries, and more. Plans start at $29 per month.

Buzzstream.
https://www.buzzstream.com/
Buzzstream is the darling of many link builders and content marketers. It is an end-to-end outreach platform, meaning it can find contact details, send emails, track relationships, and more. Buzzstream doesn't allow automatic follow ups nor one-click sending for your campaigns, so a bit of manual work is required to run campaigns through Buzzstream. Plans start at $24 per month.

Ninja Outreach

https://ninjaoutreach.com/

Ninja Outreach is another end-to-end outreach platform, including finding contact details, sending emails, personalization, automatic follow ups and more. I have noticed the majority of bloggers on this platform ask for you to pay to contribute to their site, which is a downside in my opinion. Pricing starts at $120 per month.

Pitchbox

https://pitchbox.com/

Pitchbox is an enterprise-level outreach platform, including finding contact details, personalized emails, automated follow ups, detailed reporting, and more. Pitchbox is more suited for larger teams or campaigns, SEO agencies and SEO professionals. It comes at a higher price point, but sometimes the preferred tool for serious SEO guys and gals, due to having more features and flexibility than the other platforms. Plans start at $195 per month.

ADDITIONAL LINK BUILDING OPPORTUNITIES.

The aforementioned link building techniques are enough for 99% of readers to push rankings higher than competitors. For link building junkies who've exhausted the above options, here's a handful of strategies listed in rapid-fire fashion. These are intended for advanced SEO users, who are already actively blogging and building links.

1. Create a Twitter profile.

Adding a link in a Twitter profile is a big opportunity disguised as a small opportunity. Simply by creating a Twitter profile, and listing your website in both the "website" and "bio" fields, you will get a handful of links from high domain authority aggregators that scrape your information from Twitter. Sites that do this include Klout, Twellow, and many others. To make these links more powerful, you can make your profile active without a large overhead of time. Use a service such as Hootsuite to auto-post blog posts from RSS feeds relevant to your niche, to make your profile active. Build up a base level of followers to your account with a small budget using a service like Twitter Ads.

Hootsuite
https://www.hootsuite.com/

Twitter Ads
https://ads.twitter.com

2. Pingback & trackback link building targeting authority sites.

You can get a handful of easy-win authority links, including .edu and .gov links, by linking out to blogs in your industry with pingbacks enabled. Pingbacks are notifications from your blog sent to other blogs when you mention an external post. Blogs with pingbacks enabled will show a link back to your website in their comment section when this happens.

Here's how a comment will look if it is a trackback or pingback:

Digital nomad blog
[...]read the latest tips on how to travel with only your carry on luggage[...]

Pingbacks build up valuable relevant links back to your website. They can also be a traffic source, picking up engaged readers from other sites and sending them to your site.

Run a quick search on Google to find the top 50 or top 100 blogs in your industry, then go through and find the ones with trackbacks enabled. For example, to find digital nomad blogs, you might type into Google:

intitle:"digital nomad" "comment"

Next up, in your upcoming blog posts, link out to blogs with pingbacks enabled. For this to work successfully, keep in mind you need to link out to actual posts, not the home page.

3. Create your own authority links.

The most powerful link building strategy is to simply go out and make your own authority links. By buying a previously owned website or domain, you can turn it into a blog and unlimited source for powerful, highly relevant links back to your site.

There are readers out there who will scoff at this strategy and there are readers out there nodding their heads — it's the readers nodding their heads that know how powerful this strategy is. Links from authority sources in your market are much more powerful than any other kind of link, and the easiest way to get authority links is to create your own authority site. Consider buying a website more than three or four years old with a relevant domain, for a more powerful effect.

Be careful with this strategy. If you create a network of sites like this and obscure the ownership details at the domain registry, and only link back to websites you own, you risk being labeled as the owner of a private-blog-network by Google and could receive ranking penalties. However, if you create a legitimate, authoritative resource creating genuine value for users, you should be fine.

Flippa
https://flippa.com
Market place for buying and selling websites.

Sedo
https://sedo.com
Buy and sell domains.

4. Relationship link building.

If you've been following the online advice on blogging and link building in the past couple of years you will have noticed a recurring theme: building relationships with other bloggers in your industry is a powerful way to earn strong backlinks to your site.

While this strategy is only relevant for users with active blogs on their site, fortunately, creating these relationships and getting the links is easier than it sounds. Other bloggers in your industry are just as dependent on links as you are. By linking out in your blog posts to other bloggers you 1) give a valuable backlink to the blogger, and 2) give recognition to the blogger for being an authority in the industry. Everyone likes recognition, and the law of reciprocity comes into play here, you will find most bloggers are grateful for being mentioned and happy to link back in a social media post or future blog post.

Try creating or curating popular blog posts into a top-level summary, then send a quick email to the bloggers mentioned, let them know, and very politely ask for a mention or linkback. The best part of this strategy is curating blog posts; it is often easier than creating content from scratch.

Example email:
Hey [expert blogger],
Just thought I'd give you a heads up. I've just featured you in my post [xyz]...
Hope you don't mind. If you're happy with the article, I would really appreciate a mention on social media or perhaps a link back. Or if you want anything changed, feel free to let me know.
Really enjoyed your post on [xyz].
Thanks!

Example expert round-up post:
Experienced business travellers reveal their favorite travel tips
https://www.businessinsider.com/business-travel-tips-from-expert-travelers-2015-6/?IR=T&r=SG

5. Testimonial link building.

An awesome way to get high quality, relevant links back to your site is to give out testimonials. Sometimes you can actually earn a link back to your site from somebody else's homepage, possibly one of the strongest types of links to get! I will sometimes go as far as purchasing a product just to get a testimonial link. Give this strategy a try by finding a few sites with testimonials and offering your own. Of course make it easy for the webmaster by including all the information they need, such as a photo, your name, job title, testimonial and link back to your site. The key is to look for businesses or services with a testimonials page already, or a testimonials carousel or widget on their homepage. Speed up your search with a couple of Google search queries:

"keyword" + testimonials
"keyword" + recommendations
"keyword" + "client testimonials"
"keyword" + "what customers say"

SOCIAL MEDIA & SEO.

IS SOCIAL MEDIA IMPORTANT FOR SEO?

Social media has become integral to the way we use the Internet. Important content is not only linked, it is shared, liked, tweeted and pinned. How people use the Internet has drastically changed, and this hasn't gone unnoticed over at the Googleplex. Many of the independent studies on Google's ranking algorithm show a large correlation with high-ranking pages having strong social media activity.

While the official stance from Google is that they do not directly use social signals in their algorithm, the SEO community pretty much agrees it is certainly a factor in achieving rankings. Disagreements aside, I can tell from my own experience, sites with large social followings consistently get higher rankings in a shorter timeframe.

Not only can you use social media to build social activity to increase your overall SEO strength, you can use social media to regularly create backlinks that are free and easy to build. It also increases referral traffic back to your site and engages previous customers. As a rule, social media should be a part of every SEO project, or even every marketing project.

FACEBOOK & SEO.

Facebook is the world's most popular social network. What's popular on Facebook is essentially a snapshot of public opinion, and Google have noted this by making Facebook activity a very strong factor in their algorithm. You should consider using Facebook for every SEO project. If you only have the time or budget to use one social network in your SEO strategy, use Facebook.

To improve your site's Facebook social activity, share content from your own site on your Facebook page on a regular basis.

Each time you do this, you receive more exposure from your fan base, and you also build up social activity around the content on your site. Be careful to mix this up with relevant, engaging non-commercial content for your user base, so you don't turn them off and maintain high levels of engagement. Examples include infographics, inspirational quotes, inspirational photos, and so on.

Build up your audience by including a Facebook follow button on your site, your email signatures, and your thank you or success pages.

If you want to speed up building your audience, you can use Facebook advertising to build a relevant audience of local customers. This is a good strategy if your competitors in the rankings have a larger following and you are looking to beat them. You can also use Facebook advertising to increase exposure for your posts, or even run advertising campaigns for a promotional offer. Facebook advertising stands out as a great way to build up an audience, social activity and referral sales for projects with a budget.

Facebook for business
https://www.facebook.com/business

Facebook advertising
https://www.facebook.com/business/ads

TWITTER & SEO.

Twitter is filled with discussion on the world's latest news and events. In many cases, groundbreaking news stories are released on Twitter before the world's major news outlets. The death of Osama Bin Laden is the perfect example—it was leaked on Twitter by a former chief of staff to the US Defense Secretary and within minutes it was all over the news.

Google have recognized this and use Twitter activity in their algorithm. While it may not be as strong as other social networks, you can use Twitter to build up your overall SEO strength. Twitter is a great social network to weave into your SEO strategy as you can schedule a lot of your tweets in advance without coming across as too spammy, and manage your account with only a small commitment of time and effort.

Schedule tweets to your pages such as Hootsuite and start building up your tweet counts on your pages. Mix this up with relevant and informative tweets about your industry. You should aim for a maximum of 12 tweets per day. 12 Tweets per day is roughly the limit you can post without annoying your followers. If you're lazy like me, you can schedule all of your tweets about 3 months in advance.

If you want to encourage site visitors to tweet your content for you, include a "tweet this page" link on every page or blog post on your web site.

Tweetdeck -Free
https://tweetdeck.twitter.com/

Free and easy Twitter management software. You can install Tweetdeck on your computer and manage your whole Twitter account from inside the program. Popular features include managing multiple accounts, scheduling tweets, and arranging feeds so you only see updates from Twitterers you're interested in.

Hootsuite -Free to start. $29 monthly for power users.
https://www.hootsuite.com/

More advanced than Tweetdeck, you can use Hootsuite to
schedule tweets, analyze social media traffic, manage
multiple accounts, create social media reports to monitor
your success, and much more. Recommended for power
users or automating multiple accounts.

OTHER SOCIAL NETWORKS.

Let's face it, we'd all love to play around on social
networks all day, but we don't have the spare time to be
always looking for great ideas and sharing them endlessly
on social media accounts.

If you have limited resources, focus on Facebook, Youtube
and Twitter.

If you are looking for an extra edge, doing SEO for a large
brand, or maybe you have an army of helpers waiting for
your command, you can gain significant boosts by
expanding your social activity to several social media sites.

Setup an account on the below networks, posting on the
networks most relevant to your business:

LinkedIn
https://www.linkedin.com/

LinkedIn is the Facebook for professionals. LinkedIn is a fantastic networking tool if you are in the business-to-business industry and looking to build up your personal brand or the brand of your site. If you want to increase your effectiveness on Linkedin, join groups and participate in discussions, post relevant updates about your industry and post content in the news feed.

Pinterest
https://www.pinterest.com/

Pinterest has become one of the fastest-growing social networks in a very short timeframe. Pinterest's fast-growing user base is primarily made up of women. The site has effectively turned into a giant shopping list of wish-list items. If your target audience is women, you should be on Pinterest.

Instagram
https://www.instagram.com/

Initially a mobile app to help users make their photos look pretty, Instagram has skyrocketed from a fledgling mobile app to competing with major social networks in just a few years. Instagram limits the amount of links you can post, which essentially means the links from your profile on Instagram are much more powerful. If you work in a fashion or image-heavy industry, Instagram is a must-have social network to incorporate into your SEO and overall digital strategy.

SOCIAL MEDIA ANALYTICS.

If you invest time and effort building up your social media profiles, you will want to track your results so you can separate the parts of your strategy that are successful and not so successful.

Social media analytics is different compared to other web analytics, because social analytics are geared to measuring the conversation and interaction of your fan base with your brand. Using the software listed below, you can monitor results and get valuable insights on how to improve your social media efforts:

Sprout Social - Free for 30-days. $99 per month for regular use.
https://sproutsocial.com/

Sprout Social is a great web analytics and social media management package that allows you to track the performance of your social media profiles over time. It has a free trial, suited to advanced level use and offers powerful analytic reports for major social networks.

Hootsuite - Free plan available. Paid plans start at $29 per month.
https://hootsuite.com/products/social-media-analytics

Hootsuite is quoted many times in this book and for good reason—Hootsuite is a robust social media management software allowing for control over many social networks, as well as powerful web analytics insights. Its paid plans are also quite affordable for pro-users.

Google Analytics Social Tracking - Free
https://marketingplatform.google.com/about/analytics/

Google Analytics social-tracking features are great for tracking basic social interactions that occur when visitors are on your site. It is free and includes an out-of-the-box solution with the standard setup. To see social reports, log into Google Analytics, click on the "Acquisition" tab in the main menu, then "Social."

WEB ANALYTICS IN A NUTSHELL. HOW TO MEASURE YOUR SUCCESS.

Web analytics changed how we do business in the 21st century. Now we can find valuable insights into customers previously impossible to discover, including information on website visitors' demographics, interests, online behaviors, and more. We can find out what works and what doesn't, cut underperforming marketing campaigns and increase budgets for winning campaigns. Simply put, web analytics have made it easier to grow almost any business. Read on for a quick guide covering the nuts and bolts of web analytics, and how to put web analytics to work for your business.

WHY USE GOOGLE ANALYTICS?

You may have already heard about Google Analytics. Google Analytics is the web analytics platform used by the majority of sites. It has its quirks, but it's the best readily available, all-round analytics tool available for understanding site traffic. And the best part is it's free.

If you don't have Google Analytics installed, put down this book, install Google Analytics now and then slap your web developer. I'm not joking. Without Google Analytics set up, growing a business online is like trying to pilot an airplane blindfolded. Without Google Analytics it's difficult to find out what works and what doesn't, identify issues and solve them before they turn into bigger issues, and get a sense for the general direction your business is headed. Google Analytics is usefulness for monitoring the performance of a business and is applicable to about 95% of businesses.

To get started with Google Analytics, head on over to the below URL and click on "sign in." Create a Google account if you do not have one already, and walk through the simple steps to get started. You may need help from your web developer if you are unable to edit the code on your website.

Google Analytics
https://www.google.com/analytics/

HOW TO USE GOOGLE ANALYTICS.

Let me tell you something a little risqué. On its own, most data is useless. You heard correctly, for real awareness and insights, we need to be able to compare data and identify trends over time. There are two ways to analyze and understand data in Google Analytics in reference to time:

1. Compare two date ranges.

Click on the date field input in Google Analytics. Enter two timeframes and you can compare them both. Useful date comparisons include comparing this week's performance to last week's performance, last month's performance to the month prior, and last month's performance to the same month the previous year.

2. Look at the charts over a long time frame.

Simply look at the charts over the longest time period possible and look for trends, without comparing date ranges. This is not so effective for finding hard-to-find information or identifying granular insights, but this approach is useful for a bird's eye view of the direction your traffic is heading.

Note: Seasonality is a factor affecting many businesses. Sometimes you may see a downturn in traffic, but this may not necessarily indicate your site is performing poorly. It could be that your market experiences a downward trend in certain months. If your business is experiencing a downward trend, use the "compare two date ranges" approach and compare the current month's traffic to the same month last year. If you are seeing increases, then you know your site is performing well, irrespective of seasonal trends.

ACQUISITION.

Acquisition is an area of Google Analytics any business owner or marketer should spend a lot of time reviewing. The Acquisition section of Google Analytics breaks down where your site traffic is coming from. Without keeping a close eye on your traffic sources, it is almost impossible to make informed judgments about the performance of your site or your marketing.

Click "Acquisition" in the main sidebar on the left. In the "All Traffic" section you can see actual amounts of traffic you've received from a given source. The Channels section listed under "All Traffic" is of special interest. This lists the main sources sending customers to your website. From the "Channels" tab, you can dig further for deeper insights into the performance for specific sources sending customers to your site, such as social visitors, search engine visitors, email visitors, and so on.

ORGANIC SEARCH REPORT.

The Organic Search report is essential for monitoring your performance in search engines. Within the Organic Search report, you can actually see how many times you received a visitor from a search engine.

It's worth mentioning, a few years ago Google made changes to Google Analytics that still has many search engine marketers and marketing professionals shaking their fists at the sky. Early in 2012, Google changed this tool to hide a large portion of the keyword information, making it difficult to get exact information on the keywords customers are using to arrive at your site. Thanks, Google!

Now when someone types a phrase into Google, if they are signed into a Google account while browsing, the keyword the visitor searches for will show up as a "not provided" keyword in Google Analytics report. When this happens, you have no idea what that person typed into Google before arriving at your site.

The amount of keyword information that has been obscured by Google has gradually increased, but don't be too concerned, we can still measure overall performance of search engine traffic by looking for total increases or decreases in the Organic Search report.

To view the Organic Search report, click on the Acquisition tab on the left sidebar, click on "Acquisition", "All Traffic", click on "Channels", and click on "Organic Search."

SEGMENTS.

Imagine if you could narrow down to a particular segment of your audience, such as paid traffic, search engine traffic, mobile traffic, iPad users, and so on, and instantly see how many inquiries these users have made, how much time they are spending on your site, what country they are from, and how many sales they are making. This feature exists and it is called Segments

Segments are powerful. With Segments, you can identify portions of your audience that potentially generate more inquiries or sales than other customers. You can even identify portions of your audience having difficulty using your site, and get insights to fix these areas for better performance.

To use Segments, simply click on the "Add Segment" tab at the top of every page within Google Analytics, and you can choose from the list a large number of Segments for deeper insights.

COMMON WEB ANALYTICS TERMS EXPLAINED.

Pageviews.

A Pageview is counted each time a user loads a page on your site.

Unique Pageviews.

Similar to a Pageview, but if one user loads a page several times it will only be considered one Unique Pageview.

Session.

A session is what occurs when a visitor arrives at the site, and then at some point closes the browser. If that visitor returns again, this is counted as an additional session.

User.

If a user visits your site, and then returns at a later stage, this is counted as one unique User.

Bounce Rate.

If a visitor visits your site, and then leaves without visiting any more pages, this is a bounce. The percentage of visitors who bounce is your bounce rate. A common question among marketers and business owners is: what is a good bounce rate? There is no general rule. Bounce rates vary greatly between sites and industries. If you find a particular page with a very high bounce rate (+70%), this could be an indicator the visitors do not like the content or they are experiencing technical issues.

Conversion rate.

One of the most important metrics to monitor is your site conversion rate. A conversion rate is the percentage of Users completing a desired action. The action could be filling out an inquiry form, downloading a product, or buying something from you. If you receive one hundred visitors, and three of these visitors complete a sale, this would be a three percent conversion rate.

Goals.

Goals are custom goals you can set up within Google Analytics to track particular business goals or targets you may have for your site.

Common goals to set up include newsletter signups, product downloads, inquiry form completions, and so on.

CALL TRACKING — POWERFUL ANALYTICS FOR EVERY BUSINESS.

Web analytics and VOIP tech has advanced at a lightning pace in the past few years. Tracking and attributing phone calls to marketing channels was previously an arduous task for the local or international marketer, but finally, it's now both cheap and easy to track the source of phone calls in your marketing campaigns.

Better yet, you can track your calls to a great level of detail, including discovering the source of each phone call (Google, Facebook, Google Ads, etc.) and even discover the particular keyword or ad a phone call originated from.

In case you're wondering how this wonderful technology works, most call tracking platforms use a fancy technology called "dynamic number insertion", presenting different phone numbers to different users, depending on where they came from, then tracking it in the platform and presenting the data to you, all neat-and-tidy, on a reports screen or a mobile app.

Before running through popular tools for tracking calls, let's cover important points to safeguard your search engine performance, and make sure you get setup correctly.

Key points for implementing call tracking.

1. If you rely on SEO, or local SEO, it's important to keep your "real" phone number displayed on your website, for both search users and Google-bot. Make sure your developer is aware of this, and keep your "real" number displayed at all times to these users in the call-tracking platform. If you don't do this, the "NAP" (Name, Address, Phone number) data displayed on your site could become inconsistent, and have a negative impact on search rankings.

2. Make sure the call tracking platform integrates with Google Ads and Google Analytics.

3. If you're using a CRM system, like Salesforce and so on, you might want to check the call tracking system links up with your particular CRM.

4. Finally, if you're on WordPress, or another CMS, ensure the call tracking platform has a plugin for your particular CMS for easy setup. If the platform has a plugin for the software running your site, this often means you can get setup in under an hour or so.

Popular call tracking platforms on the market right now.

Call Rail
https://www.callrail.com/
Call Rail is popular for its ease-of-use, international support, integrations with Google Analytics, Google Ads, WordPress, Salesforce and flexibility. It also includes cool features like text messaging, geo-routing, voicemail and more. Plans start at $45 per month.

Call Tracking Metrics

https://www.calltrackingmetrics.com/

Call Tracking Metrics is another popular platform, also offering international support, Google Analytics, Google Ads, WordPress integrations, and overall, similar features to Call Rail. Some online user reports mention preferring Call Rail for its simplicity and flexibility, and found Call Tracking Metrics a little difficult to navigate, but in the end, it's often best to trial both platforms initially and see what works best for your business. Plans start at $39 per month.

OTHER WEB ANALYTICS TOOLS.

There are many web analytics tools out there to help with improving the performance of your site. Google Analytics is great for understanding overall traffic performance, but if you want to delve deeper, check out the following tools for greater insights:

Crazy Egg - Free to start. Plants start at $24 per month. https://www.crazyegg.com/

If you want a visual indication of how visitors behave on your site once they arrive, Crazy Egg is a fantastic tool. With Crazy Egg, you can get heat maps of where visitors click on the page. You can also see heat maps of how far visitors scroll down the page.

Visual Website Optimizer – 30 day free trial.
https://vwo.com/

Visual Website Optimizer is a popular split-testing analytics tool. With Visual Website Optimizer, you can split test different variations of your site, and see which version makes more sales or conversions, and increase your overall sales.

Google Tag Assistant
https://get.google.com/tagassistant/

Google Tag Assistant is a handy free tool, for diagnosing any issues with the tracking codes for all the fancy web tracking tools you've setup on your site. It's especially useful for developers diagnosing issues, when you're having obvious problems with your web analytics.

Google Data Studio
https://datastudio.google.com/overview

If you're a data junky then you'll get your fix with Google Data Studio. Data Studio is hardcore, it can create visual reports so you can monitor almost anything—calls, ad campaigns on various platforms, search rankings, Salesforce leads, your bookkeeping system, the list goes on. The best part is, it's free.

TROUBLESHOOTING COMMON SEO PROBLEMS & HOW TO FIX THEM.

Dealing with Google can be massively frustrating at times. Customer support barely exists, and trying to understand why your site isn't playing well with Google can spiral into a wild goose chase.

Don't let Google's lack of customer support or the horror stories dishearten you. Most of the time, if a site is experiencing Google problems, it is only temporary. SEO problems are rarely irrecoverable.

Usually it's simply a matter of finding out the underlying cause of the problem — more often than not, the cause isn't what the popular blog posts are saying it might be. This sometimes means fixing several items. Once all fixed, you have stacked the deck in your favor and you are more likely to make a speedy recovery.

This chapter outlines common SEO problems that plague web site owners.

If you are not at all technically inclined, I urge you to read the section on getting additional advice, or even consider getting professional help if your site is experiencing serious SEO issues.

WHAT TO DO WHEN YOUR SITE IS NOT LISTED IN GOOGLE AT ALL.

This is a common problem among webmasters and business owners alike.

If you have just launched a brand-new site, it is possible Google has not crawled your site yet. You can do a quick spot check by typing "site:yoursiteaddress.com" into the Google search bar and checking to see if your site comes up at all. If it doesn't, it's possible Google's spider hasn't crawled your site and doesn't know it exists.

Typically, all that's required for Google to pick up your site is to generate a handful of links to your site and some social activity.

Tweeting a link to your site is a quick way to ensure your site is indexed by Google's software, typically within 24 hours. Try to share your site from a handful of social networks for faster results.

Check Google again in 24 hours with the "site:www.yoursite…" search query and see if any pages from your site come up. If you do see pages, this means Google has indexed your site.

If this doesn't work, ask your web designer to setup Google Search Console for you, login and see if there are any errors. If there are errors, Google will outline the steps to fix them, so Google can see your site.

Google Search Console's handy URL inspection tool is great for troubleshooting and finding issues. It confirms if your page is supported by Google, not suffering from any penalties, successfully appearing in the index, is mobile friendly and more. To access the URL inspection tool, click "URL inspection" in the left sidebar in Google Search Console.

Google Search Console
https://www.google.com/webmasters/

WHAT TO DO WHEN YOUR BUSINESS IS NOT RANKING FOR YOUR OWN BUSINESS NAME.

A business not coming up in the top position in Google for searches for the official business name is a surprisingly common issue among brand new sites. Google is smart, but sometimes you need to give Google a nudge to associate your new site with the name of your brand.

This solution is easily fixed by building links to your site, with some of the links with your brand name as the anchor text. This can take up to a couple of weeks for Google to see these links, connect the dots and realize your site is the real deal.

The fast way to get the ball rolling is to do a quick search for the business directories used in your country — Whitepages, Yellow Pages, Yelp, and so on — fill out a listing for your business on each site and include a link back to your web site. The more links the better, but you should be aiming for a minimum of 50 links. In 95% of cases, this will solve the problem of a site not coming up in the top results of searches for the business name.

If this doesn't work, setup Facebook and Twitter accounts for your business, filling out as much information about your business as possible in the profile. Then do a post a day for about two weeks, mixing in links to your site in the posts.

If you still can't get your site ranking high enough, use Link Explorer to spy on competing sites ranking higher for the brand name. Do their pages have more backlinks than the total amount of links to your site? If this is the case, you are going to need to build more links.

WHAT TO DO WHEN YOUR RANKINGS HAVE DROPPED OFF.

Here's a sad truth about SEO: if you achieve a top ranking, it may not keep its position forever. There are billions of web pages competing for top positions in Google. New sites are being created every day. It requires an ongoing effort to keep pages ranking high.

If your rankings have dropped off from the top position and slowly moving their way down the search results, it's possible you've been affected by a Google update or spam filter. Read through the Google Updates chapter later in this book, and also look through the additional resources for keeping updated on new Google updates in the same chapter.

On the other hand, it's more likely your competitors have simply acquired more links or more social activity than your site. Use Link Explorer to spy on competitors, find out how many backlinks they have, how much social media activity they have, and set these amounts as your target to build your rankings back up.

Next, it's time to start a link building campaign with the targeted keywords as outlined in the chapter on link building.

HOW TO SEEK PROFESSIONAL HELP FOR FREE.

Finding the right SEO help can be frustrating for site owners. There is a lot of information to navigate, with varying levels of quality and accuracy. It's difficult to get in touch with SEO practitioners at the top of their field.

That said, there are sites that can put your questions in front of world-leading experts of almost any topic for free. Use the below sites for highly technical responses, and you can create an army of Internet experts to try to solve your problem for you.

The key to success with the below resources is to be specific. The more specific you are, and the more information you provide, you increase your chances you will receive a detailed answer that will point you in the right direction.

For greater results, post your question on *all* of the sites below, and sit back and wait for the answers to come in. You will get more answers and will be in a better position to consider which solution is best.

Moz Q&A
https://moz.com/community/q

Moz's Q&A forums used to be private, but were eventually recently released to the public. Here you can speak with a large number of SEO professionals directly and attract high quality answers to your questions. Great for SEO specific problems.

Pro Webmasters
https://webmasters.stackexchange.com/

The Pro Webmasters Q&A board can have your questions answered by webmasters of high-performing sites.

Quora
https://www.quora.com/

Quora is an all-round Q&A posting board, where you can get a question answered on almost anything. On Quora, questions are sometimes answered by high-profile experts. Marketers, business owners, you name it, there are many leading industry authorities posting answers to questions on Quora.

Wordpress Answers
https://wordpress.stackexchange.com/

If your site is built on Wordpress, it's inevitable you will eventually encounter some kind of technical hurdle. The Wordpress Answers Q&A board is a great resource to seek out help.

LOCAL SEO. SEO FOR LOCAL BUSINESSES.

WHY USE LOCAL SEO?

Unless you have been living under a rock, you have seen listings for local businesses appearing at the top of search results in Google and Google Maps. Local listings – previously known as Google Place page listings, then rebranded as Google+ pages, now known as Google My Business listings – however they will be titled next, they are a powerful marketing tool for small businesses.

Let's look at some statistics, the following facts were discovered in several recent studies on the behavior of local customers.

- 97% of search engine users searched online to find a local business.
- 76% of consumers who conducted a local search on their smartphone visited a store within a day.
- 78% of local mobile searches lead to an in-store purchase.

12 Local SEO Stats Every Business Owner and Marketer Should Know in 2019 – Social Media Today https://www.socialmediatoday.com/news/12-local-seo-stats-every-business-owner-and-marketer-should-know-in-2019-i

Holy mackerel, if you are a local business owner and those figures aren't making your jaw drop, I don't know what will. Now that we know if you own a local business, local search can be the Yoko Ono to your John Lennon, let's delve deeper and find out what makes a local search result.

Local search results differ from traditional organic search results by representing a local business instead of a normal web page, and appearing at the top of the search results and on map listings.

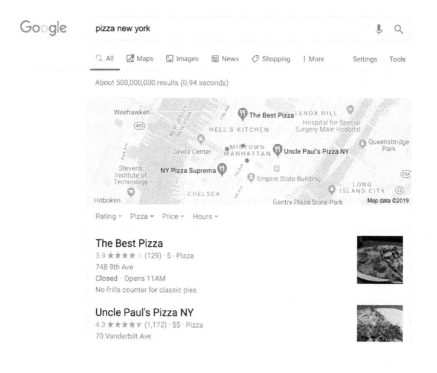

Users can get business contact details, opening hours and reviews and find the information they need quickly and easily, instead of having to dig around a clunky business site.

The local listings can be a powerful tool to attract traffic. In many cases, local listings can lead to many more inquiries than regular SEO rankings. But does this mean you should scrap traditional SEO in favor of local SEO? Nope. You can do both and potentially double the amount of potential traffic you can receive.

HOW TO RANK HIGH WITH LOCAL SEO.

Ranking high with local SEO takes a different approach than traditional SEO. Google's algorithm is looking for a different set of signals to determine the popularity of a business to decide how high to rank it in the search results.

If you think about it, if a restaurant is really popular in a city, a whole bunch of links from all over the world probably isn't the best factor to determine how valuable the business is to the local area.

A better indicator of the importance would be mentions of the business's name and phone number across the web, customer reviews, and details on the website that show the business is based in the area being searched.

Below is a list of the most important ranking factors Google use for local listings:

1. Google My Business Signals (Proximity to searcher, correct categories, keyword in business title, etc.)
2. Link Signals (Inbound anchor text, linking domain authority, linking domain quantity, etc.)
3. Review Signals (Review quantity, review velocity, review diversity, etc.)
4. On-Page Signals (Presence of NAP, keywords in titles, domain authority, etc.)
5. Citation Signals (NAP consistency, citation volume, etc.)
6. Behavioral Signals (Click-through rate, mobile clicks to call, check-ins, etc.)
7. Personalization.
8. Social Signals (Google engagement, Facebook engagement, Twitter engagement, etc.)

These are the strongest factors fetched from Moz's annual Local Search Ranking Factors survey. If you want to rank high in the local search results, all you have to do is ensure your site and Google My Business page have more of these features than your competitors.

For a complete breakdown of local SEO ranking factors, visit the below link, where the world's leading authorities on local SEO publish an industry survey on the local ranking factors every year.

Moz's Local Search Ranking Factors
https://moz.com/local-search-ranking-factors

GETTING STARTED WITH LOCAL SEO.

To get started, the first step is to create your business page on Google My Business. Visit the URL below and complete every area of your profile as possible. This means creating a detailed description of your business, available payment methods, and so on. The more information you complete, the more you increase your chances of ranking your page higher.

Google My Business
https://www.google.com/business

When creating your business listing, make sure you choose the most accurate category for your business, e.g. if you provide plumbing as a service, you want to choose "plumbing" as your category, not "trades" or "home repairs."

BUILDING CITATIONS.

Citations are the links of local SEO. A citation occurs each time your name, address, phone number (NAP) is mentioned on the web. The more citations you have, the more likely your site will rank high. The easiest places to build citations are the many local business directories available for businesses.

While there's many online directories for creating business listings, the following websites would be a good start for a US-based business.

https://www.facebook.com/business
https://www.linkedin.com/
https://www.yellowpages.com/
https://biz.yelp.com/
https://www.local.com/
https://www.whitepages.com/business
https://www.manta.com/
http://www.citysearch.com
https://foursquare.com/business/
https://www.merchantcircle.com/

BUILDING REVIEWS.

Citations and reviews are the link building of local SEO. If you are only building citations, you only have half of the equation covered. To rank highly, you need to ensure your business accumulates online reviews.

Many businesses struggle with this. This is because it's tough to get customers to fill out reviews! You have to make it easy for your customers.

Include links to your business Google My Business page on your site, email signatures, flyers, and business cards, prompting customers to leave a review. Encourage customers at the end of each sale or transaction to leave a review. By creating every opportunity possible for customers to leave a review, you can significantly increase reviews.

But whatever you do, don't buy reviews. This is a quick way to get into Google's naughty books. Purchased reviews can be picked up by Google's filters and are likely to be excluded from your business profile anyways.

Feeling lazy to hire a graphic designer? No problem! Google created an awesome tool that generates free posters, signs, and stickers to put in your store and encourage more reviews from customers. Check it out at the following URL.

Google My Business Marketing Kit – Think With Google https://marketingkit.withgoogle.com/

SUPERCHARGING LOCAL SEO WITH PHOTOS AND VIDEOS.

For better or worse, for many people, taking selfies and photos of what they're eating for dinner has become a daily habit—and it comes with no surprise Google are capitalizing on this ubiquitous trend. Late August 2017, Google enabled video and uploads from the general public to Google Business listings on Google Maps. An underused marketing opportunity flying under the radar—for now—and a savvy local business owner can use this to their advantage.

Why are photos and videos important for a local business?

Whether or not the number of photos and video's uploaded to a Google Business listing is a ranking factor is unknown—it wouldn't be surprising if it is, it would be a solid indicator of the popularity and activity of a local business. But you can be sure Google will stay tight-lipped on the matter. Either way, the more photos and videos uploaded to your Google Business page will lead to higher user-engagement with your profile, which will likely lead to higher rankings.

But the real advantage lies in enticing more customers to your business through imagery. Ever heard the phrase, "a picture is worth a thousand words?" Customers researching a local restaurant, cafe or hotel are heavily focused on photos when deciding where to go. Just look at your own experience—ever taken a peek at the photos and videos of a restaurant or hotel, and a particular photo put you over the edge? If you haven't included photos and videos in your local SEO efforts, you're missing out on a piece of the pie. Here's two simple approaches to get amongst the action.

1. Encourage customers to share their experience at your business.

Encouraging customers to share their experience at your business with a photo or video is an effective way to build up authentic photos associated with your page. It'll build up the perceived popularity of your business too. Why not take it to the next level, and entice customers with a free drink or discount off their meal by sharing their experience?

For the general public to upload photos or videos, all they need to do is tap on your listing on Google Maps, scroll down and click "add a photo", and done! Official guide by Google listed below.

Add, Remove, or Share Photos and Videos – Google Maps Help
https://support.google.com/maps/answer/2622947

2. Add photos and videos to your business profile yourself.

If you're running a restaurant, hotel, cafe, or any other local-type business for that matter, you should have a handful of professional-looking photos uploaded to your profile at a bare minimum — so customers know what to look forward to when visiting your business, or what they're missing out on…

Fortunately, adding photos and videos to your Google Business profile is easy as pie. Simply log in to Google My Business, click photos on the left menu and upload away. For additional documentation, check out the official guide from Google HQ below.

Add Local Business Photos - Google My Business Help
https://support.google.com/business/answer/6103862

LOCAL SEO RANKING CHECKLIST & ESSENTIAL RESOURCES.

While looking at your local competitors and working to beat them is probably the best overall strategy, progressing through the following checklist will put you on your way to ranking high at the top of the local search results.

1. Verify your business profile on Google My Business.
2. Fill out as much information as possible on your Google My Business profile, including description, category associations, images and videos.
3. Include your business name and location somewhere on your website, this could be your contact page or home page.
4. Include your full business name, address and phone somewhere on your site, these should be grouped together so Google will register it as a citation.
5. Include the appropriate schema.org tags in your website markup, following their specification for local businesses at the following URL.

Schema.org Local Business Specifications.
https://schema.org/LocalBusiness
6. Encourage customers to review your business.
7. Submit your website to the major business directories like Yelp, Yellow Pages, CitySearch and so on. You can use tools like Moz Local to submit your business to all of the major directories in one go.
Moz Local.
https://moz.com/local
8. Cross-check your business listings for correct NAP data. These details need to be consistent across your Google My Business listing, website contact page, and external business listings.

A downloadable copy of the above steps is also available in the SEO checklist at the end of the book.

Essential local SEO resources for keeping up to date.

Just like traditional SEO, local SEO constantly changes and becomes more complex over time. To keep your skills sharp you need to stay up to date with the latest knowledge in the industry. The resources below should be considered essential reading for anyone looking to hone their local SEO skill set.

Local SEO Guide

https://www.localseoguide.com/

Andrew Shotland's Local SEO Guide is an enduring commentary of local SEO techniques and updates in the industry. His useful blog has been around for as long as local SEO has been a thing and popular among the SEO community for good reason — the blog's regular contributions and willingness to give away valuable and actionable advice.

Moz Local Learning Center

https://moz.com/learn/local

The pre-eminent pundits at Moz have compiled a very useful and detailed guide for managing all aspects of local marketing. Their guide is both extensive and easy to read, making it a great resource for both beginners and advanced practitioners.

HOW TO DOMINATE SEARCH WITH RICH RESULTS. STRUCTURED DATA, JSON-LD, FACEBOOK OPEN GRAPH & MORE.

WHAT ARE RICH SNIPPETS?

Ever searched in Google and saw a ginormous ranking just above the search results?... These large search results are called "rich snippets" and can send a mind-blowing amount of traffic.

Before I jump into techniques, still not sure what I'm talking about? Quickly Google a couple of questions and look for the giant search result at the top of the results, you can't miss it — it's only four times bigger than a regular search result. Here's example searches that usually deliver a rich snippet in the results, "what are rich snippets", "how to get started in real estate", "how to increase your blog traffic", and so on...

WHY YOU NEED TO FOCUS ON RICH RESULTS.

Considering banging your head against the wall, wondering why you're reading such a soul-destroying dry topic? Well, don't throw this book out the window just yet...

These new technologies allow greater control over search listings, making it easier for search engines to crawl your site, potentially featuring your content as a "rich result", helping you get higher click-through rates and get more eyeballs on content. Think of this technology like meta tags on steroids…

If that hasn't got your appetite going, simply put, targeting rich snippets can send a ton of traffic. According to a study by Ahrefs, featured snippets always get more traffic than first search results — if you can occupy both the rich snippet position and #1 result, you can get 31% more traffic than occupying just the #1 position… Pretty neat, huh?

Still not convinced?.. With voice search predicted to be 50% of searches by the end of 2020 by Comscore, and 40% of voice search results originating from rich results, targeting rich-results is a must — if you want to get amongst the rising voice search trend.

WHY USE STRUCTURED DATA AND JSON-LD?

To tell Google which parts of your content you want considered for a rich result, you need to use code called "structured data." With new technologies, as always, there's a debate about the best to use — JSON-LD, RDFa, microdata, the list goes on…

I won't waste your time with a technical debate. Google has openly stated JSON-LD is their preferred code — and made it clear not to mix structured data technologies for fear of confusing their spider…

We're here for high rankings and traffic, not a lengthy diatribe on each individual technology, so let's go with what Google recommends for the purposes of this book — JSON-LD.

HOW TO GET STARTED WITH JSON-LD.

So, what does all this JSON-LD structured data stuff look like? Let's look at   a business listing to see how it should be coded, according to Google's recommendations.

```
<script type="application/ld+json">
{
  "@context": "https://schema.org",
  "@type": "Organization",
  "url": "http://www.example.com",
  "name": "Unlimited Ball Bearings Corp.",
  "contactPoint": {
    "@type": "ContactPoint",
    "telephone": "+1-401-555-1212",
    "contactType": "Customer service"
  }
}
</script>
```

You can see how the JSON-LD example code from Google gives the search engine a friendly nudge to recognize the information as a business listing, such as the name and the phone number.

While the above example will be just enough if you have a simple business listing, you or your developer will have to use Google's documentation and tools, listed later in this chapter, to ensure your code is implemented correctly.

Different Types of Rich Results Supported by Google.

Google supports the below rich results. If you have any of these content types on your site, you can benefit from Google's recommended additional code.

- Article
- Book
- Breadcrumb

- Carousel
- Course
- Critic review
- Dataset
- Employer Aggregate Rating
- Event
- Fact Check
- FAQ
- How-to
- Job Posting
- Job Training (beta)
- Local Business Listing
- Logo
- Movie
- Occupation
- Product
- Q&A
- Recipe
- Review snippet
- Sitelinks Searchbox
- Software App (beta)
- Speakable (news content)
- Subscription and paywalled content
- Video

Holy cow! That's a lot of different search result types. Fortunately, Google have listed them neatly with example code at the following page.

Search Gallery of Structured Data – Google
https://developers.google.com/search/docs/guides/search-gallery

When you or your developer are testing the code on your site, use Google's Structured Data Testing Tool and make sure the code is implemented correctly. Finally, use Google's Rich Results Test and preview how your page can appear in the search results.

Structured Data Testing Tool - Google
https://search.google.com/structured-data/testing-tool

Rich Results Test – Google
https://search.google.com/test/rich-results

HOW TO TARGET FEATURED SNIPPET RANKINGS IN GOOGLE'S SEARCH RESULTS.

After you've uploaded a bunch of fancy JSON-LD code into your site, you're probably wondering when you appear at the top of the results... Using JSON-LD is just one step, if you want to achieve the coveted featured snippet ranking, you'll need to satisfy the following requirements.

1. Rank on the first page, first. Almost all featured snippets are fetched from rankings on the first page. Follow techniques from the On-Page SEO and Link building chapter and work your way up the results first.

2. Create "snippet bait" targeting 40-50 words. SEMrush did a giant study on rich results and featured snippets, finding almost all text-based rich snippets range between 40 to 50 words.

3. Structure your content to target featured snippets. Hint: putting target keywords as H2 or H3 headings, followed with clear and concise paragraphs around 40-50 words, is a solid approach.

5. Use images. Featured snippets often contain images, I like to call them "snimmages" — for some reason, this terminology never really caught on like I hoped... Using images increases chances for both text and images appearing in the featured snippet. According to Google's official guidelines, images should be at least 1200 pixels wide. And using multiple high-resolution images with aspect ratios 16x9, 4x3, and 1x1 can help with appearing on different devices.

HOW TO TARGET "PEOPLE ALSO ASK" AND QUESTION-BASED RICH RESULTS.

There's another popular type of rich snippet appearing for almost any question type search—the "People also ask" rich snippet. Fortunately, some clever SEOs have figured out general techniques for targeting these sexy rankings.

1. Your desired ranking must be a question type keyword. Searches not phrased as a question won't always trigger a "People always ask" snippet, best focus on question type keywords.

2. Your answer should be clear and concise. Well-written and clear answers have a much greater chance of being featured then poorly written answers. Remember the 40-50 words technique from earlier in this chapter.

3. Include a Q&A or how-to section on your site. Increase content in a question and answer format and increase your odds of being featured for question-type searches.

4. Provide more valuable information than a simple and direct answer. If your answer has numbered lists, rich media such as images and videos, and is generally more helpful than an obvious answer to the question, then you have a greater chance of being featured.

5. Add Google's recommended question-type JSON-LD code to relevant pages... While this won't guarantee results, it'll encourage Google to look at your pages and consider them for use in the rich results. Recommended JSON-LD code is listed at each of the following pages.

FAQ – Structured Data, Google Search
https://developers.google.com/search/docs/data-types/faqpage

How-to – Structured Data, Google Search
https://developers.google.com/search/docs/data-types/how-to

Q&A – Structured Data, Google Search
https://developers.google.com/search/docs/data-types/qapage

VOICE SEARCH SEO AND GOOGLE'S SPEAKABLE STRUCTURED DATA.

With the rise of miniature circular voice speaking robots invading people's homes—virtual assistants like Alexa and Google Assistant—it comes with little surprise Google are making moves to capture this market, and you can too!

Before we cover Google's "Speakable" markup, and how any business can optimize for voice search, you might be wondering why voice search is important—after all, you want customers to land on your site, not spoken aloud, right?

Not necessarily... If voice searchers find a solid voice answer, they are likely to visit your site. Voice search is an upward trend and best viewed as an additional source of traffic, not something that will take away from current traffic. Now we've established it's worthwhile putting voice search optimization on the radar, lets jump into the gritty details.

Implementing Speakable for US based news publishers.

Implementing Speakable is straightforward. Firstly, you need to be a US based news publisher. Secondly, you need to submit your site for consideration in Google's Publisher Center. Finally, you will need to direct your site developer to review Schema.org's technical guidelines and implement their code on your site. Review the following resources and get started.

Google - Speakable and Submission for Eligibility
https://developers.google.com/search/docs/data-types/speakable#eligibility

Schema.org - Speakable Developer Documentation
https://schema.org/speakable

Voice Search Optimization for regular site owners and marketers.

We're not all US-based news publishers and it's understandable regular site owners and marketers want to jump on the voice search bandwagon. While voice search optimization is new, a handful of techniques have been established by industry insiders. Implement these and you will increase chances of having your words of wisdom echoed by a voice speaking robot in a stranger's home.

- Short answers in substantial content… Pages with over 2000 words appear more frequently in search results than articles 500 or so words. Within long-form content, include short-form content, in a question and answer format, using short and concise answers, following the 40-50 word rule mentioned earlier.
- 65% of voice search results use HTTPS and have SSL certificates installed… If you've read this far and haven't installed an SSL certificate, I'm starting to get a little concerned.
- Focus on building an authoritative site in your niche — relevant links, high value content, active social profiles, and so on.

- Make sure your website loads fast—4.6 seconds or faster to be precise. A large portion of voice searches are performed on mobile devices with slow Internet connections.

Check out Neil Patel's quick and dirty VSO guide for more practical tips.

Neil Patel - 3 SEO Tips for Voice Search Optimization
https://www.youtube.com/watch?v=UpaOahLBmFQ

FACEBOOK OPEN GRAPH.

While we know schema.org is the best approach for adding meta data to your site, there is one additional meta data technology you should also use.

Facebook's Open Graph language allows you to determine how your site listing appears when shared on Facebook.

If you do not include Facebook's Open Graph code on your site, when a user shares your content on Facebook it will show a plain listing on the news feed, with the responsibility on the user to describe the article and make it worth reading. If you include Facebook Open Graph code, it comes up looking sexy, just like your search listings if you have been using your meta title and meta description tags correctly.

By putting your best foot forward, and making your listing show up correctly on Facebook, you will encourage more customers to click to your site and increase the amount of likes and shares of your page. This will increase the social signals of the page.

Here's an example of properly formatted meta code using Facebook Open Graph. As you can see, there are only minor tweaks required to make your page show up nicely on Facebook's news feed. So go ahead and use it on your site!

```
<title>Buy Baseball Jackets Online</title>
<meta property='og:type' content='site'>
<meta property-'og:description' name='description'
content='Wide range of Baseball Jackets online, for all
leagues and players. Free delivery and free returns both-
ways in USA.'/>
```

If you're worried about confusing search engines by using several "structured data" technologies at the same time, such as Open Graph and schema.org, don't worry, you won't have any problems.

Facebook Open Graph is mainly used by Facebook's web crawler, not by search engines, so you can use Open Graph and schema.org in tandem without any problems.

If you want to read up further on Facebook's Open Graph, or if you have complex types of listings on your site, checkout Facebook's Open Graph guide below.

Open Graph Protocol
https://ogp.me/

POWERFUL SEO TOOLS.

The following tools can help find link building opportunities, diagnose site issues, create easy-to-understand SEO reports, make Google crawl your site faster and much more. Ultimately, the below tools make it easier to achieve high rankings, and can potentially save hours, days or even weeks of time.

Are there more SEO tools out there than in this list? Sure. SEO tools are a dime a dozen. The following is a selection of the tools I have found useful and to list out the tools mentioned in this book, for ease of reference. Some are free, some are paid, but most offer a free trial long enough to start optimizing your site. I have no affiliation with any of these sites, I've just listed tools that I find useful. So, jump in and have fun.

RESEARCH TOOLS.

KWfinder
https://kwfinder.com/

KWFinder is a fairly new research tool to the market, providing traffic data for keywords, estimated SEO difficulty, competitive data on sites ranking in the top 10, and much more. Its well-rounded feature set means you could use this tool alone for your keyword research without having to use multiple tools. Plans start at $29.

Google Ads Keyword Planner
https://ads.google.com/home/tools/keyword-planner/

The Google Ads Keyword Planner has been mentioned several times throughout this book for good reason, it allows you to download estimated traffic for keywords users are typing into Google's search box — powerful knowledge to have in your SEO toolkit. You can see how many times a keyword has been searched in Google, you can also narrow this down by country and even device type, including mobile phones and so on. During recent years, Google have clamped down on the free data available to non-paying users, to access all the research data you will need an active Google Ads campaign and must be regularly spending at least a modest amount of money.

Google Trends -Free
https://www.google.com/trends/

Google Trends provides powerful stats of search trends over time. Great for seeing how your market performs overall, and how demand changes over time for your keywords.

Moz - Free and Paid.
https://moz.com/free-seo-tools

No book on SEO would ever be complete without a mention of Moz. Moz offers keyword analysis, brand monitoring, rankings tracking, on-page SEO suggestions, search engine crawl tests, and much more. An essential toolbox for every SEO practitioner, from beginner to advanced.

SEOQuake - Free
https://www.seoquake.com/

The SEOQuake toolbar gives you a powerful set of stats for any site you visit, right within your browser.

SEOQuake also has a great option that gives you the important stats for pages ranking in Google's search results. A great tool for snooping on competitors and doing market research.

SEOQuake's powerful toolbar works on Google Chrome, Safari & Firefox.

Ubersuggest - Free
https://neilpatel.com/ubersuggest/

Automatically download the auto-suggested keywords from Google's search results for a nice, juicy collection of long-tail keywords.

LSIGraph: LSI Keyword Generator
https://lsigraph.com/

Generate semantic, long-tail and LSI keyword suggestions. Great for both SEO and PPC campaigns.

OPTIMIZATION TOOLS.

Google Page Speed Insights - Free
https://developers.google.com/speed/pagespeed/insights

Google Page Speed Insights is a fantastic tool provided by Google to help speed up your site. Google Page Speed Insights will give you a score on how well your load time is performing, and provide a simple set of suggestions to forward to your developers and speed up your site.

Google Snippet Optimization Tool - Free
https://www.seomofo.com/snippet-optimizer.html

This handy little tool lets you type out title tags and meta tags and see a live preview of how your site will appear in the search engines.

Google Search Console - Free
https://search.google.com/search-console/welcome

Google Search Console is another great tool, and if you haven't got Google Search Console set up, drop what you are doing and set it up now!

Google Search Console will report urgent messages if there are any severe problems when Google comes along and crawls your site. You can also submit your sitemap directly to Google from within Google Search Console, meaning you know Google has been given a friendly nudge to come around and pick up all the content on your site. This is a must-have SEO tool for every site.

HTTP Status Code Checker
https://httpstatus.io/

If you have ever setup a URL redirect, or asked your developer to, it's always a good idea to check and ensure the redirect has been setup correctly.

Use the redirect checker to make sure your redirects are returning successful responses to the web browser, so you can feel confident Google is picking it up properly too.

Lighthouse – Tools For Web Developers – Google
https://developers.google.com/web/tools/lighthouse/

Lighthouse provides reports on website performance, accessibility, adherence to programming best practices, SEO and more—with actionable steps on improving each of these areas. Lighthouse is best suited for advanced developers working on complicated projects, opposed to finding easily identifiable improvements for simple websites.

Robots.txt Analyzer - Free
http://tools.seobook.com/robots-txt/analyzer/

Many robots.txt files can often have slight errors that are difficult to pick up, especially for larger sites. Run your robots.txt file through this tool for a free analysis to see if there are any errors.

Robots.txt Generator -Free
http://www.yellowpipe.com/yis/tools/robots.txt/

If you're lazy like I am, you'll love this free robots.txt generator. Works great for the most basic or advanced robots.txt users to create robots.txt files quickly and easily.

Schema Creator - Free
https://www.schemaapp.com/

Great and easy-to-use tool to automatically generate your schema.org markup.

Pingdom Website Speed Test - Free
https://tools.pingdom.com/

The Pingdom Website Speed Test is a great tool for monitoring how quickly your site is loading, and find opportunities to make it load even faster.

With the Pingdom Speed test you can see how fast your site loads, and how large the files are on your site. You can easily find the large files on your site that are chewing up resources and bloating your load time.

Test My Site - Think With Google
https://testmysite.thinkwithgoogle.com/

This tool is both easy-to-use and indispensable for finding easy-win load speed improvements for mobile users—and handy for seeing how your site performs compared to competitors.

Fortunately, the handy tool provides free reports and if you follow the recommendations and get your site performing better than competitors, you can make out like a bandit in the search results.

Xenu's Link Sleuth - Free
http://home.snafu.de/tilman/xenulink.html

Don't be put off by the old-school design on the page that offers this very powerful SEO-tool for free.

Xenu's Link Sleuth is one of the most powerful SEO-tools available, that will crawl your entire site, or a list of links, and offer very powerful and juicy stats for each of your pages, such as stats on which pages have 404 errors, 301 redirects, server errors, title tags, meta desc tags, the list goes on! This tool has been around for years, and is a must-have tool for the more advanced SEO practitioner.

XML Sitemaps - Free to trial. $19.99 for large sites. https://www.xml-sitemaps.com/

XML Sitemaps is a fantastic tool for creating an XML sitemap to submit to Google. Useful for sites that do not have a built in XML sitemap functionality.

The tool automatically formats the sitemap so it is in the right format for Google and other search engines. With XML Sitemaps you can create a sitemap for your site within minutes.

LINK BUILDING TOOLS.

Link Clump
https://github.com/benblack86/linkclump

Possibly one of my favorite tools. Link Clump is a free Chrome extension that allows you to highlight and copy all the links on the page in one click. Great for copying the Google search results into a spreadsheet, without having to individually visit each page.

Ahrefs Backlink Checker – Free to try, then $99 per month.
https://www.ahrefs.com/

Ahrefs offers probably one of the most up-to-date indexes of links pointing to websites, and a highly accurate tool for analyzing links pointing to your site – and to your competitors. It also offers other competitive data, like keyword suggestions and estimated traffic numbers, so you can be sneaky and copy keyword ideas from your competitors.

Buzzstream - Free trial. $24 per month starter plan available.
https://www.buzzstream.com/

Buzzstream helps you find linkbuilding opportunities and conduct link outreach campaigns. Buzzstream will even find the contact details on the site for you.

Hunter
https://hunter.io/
Hunter is purely focused on finding contact details and is very good at it. It has a nice Chrome plugin that shows you the all the contact details it can find for a particular site while browsing. Free plans include up to 100 contact information requests, for more contact requests plans start at $49 per month.

Mailshake
https://mailshake.com

Mailshake is pure-outreach. You will need to provide
contact information yourself. It is effective at sending
personalized email campaigns, and you can import all the
personalization info including name, address and a
personal message via csv file. Includes automatic follow-
ups, email template libraries, and more. Plans start at $39
per month.

Buzzstream.
https://www.buzzstream.com/

Buzzstream is the darling of many link builders and
content marketers. It is an end-to-end outreach platform,
meaning it can find contact details, send emails, track
relationships, and more. Buzzstream doesn't allow
automatic follow-ups nor one-click sending for your
campaigns, so a bit of manual work is required to run
campaigns through Buzzstream. Plans start at $24 per
month.

Ninja Outreach
https://ninjaoutreach.com/
Ninja Outreach is another end-to-end outreach platform,
including finding contact details, sending emails,
personalization, automatic follow-ups and more. I have
noticed the majority of bloggers on this platform ask for
you to pay to contribute to their site, which is a downside
in my opinion. Pricing starts at $120 per month.

Pitchbox

https://pitchbox.com/

Pitchbox is an enterprise-level outreach platform, including finding contact details, personalized emails, automated follow-ups, detailed reporting, and more. Pitchbox is more suited for larger teams or campaigns, SEO agencies and SEO professionals. It comes at a higher price point, but it is sometimes the preferred tool for serious SEO guys and gals, due to having more features and flexibility than the other platforms. Plans start at $195 per month.

Moz - Link Explorer - Free for limited access. $99 per month for pro users.

https://moz.com/link-explorer

Link Explorer is a must for understanding the links pointing to your site and competitors' sites. Cheeky little tricks with Link Explorer include exporting competitors' backlinks and looking over these links for opportunities to build links to your site. For higher level of detail, I do prefer Ahrefs when it comes to analyzing links, but a paid-membership for Link Explorer also gives you access to Moz's entire suite of SEO tools.

WEB ANALYTICS TOOLS.

Google Analytics
https://analytics.google.com/analytics/web/

Google Analytics is the market leader in web analytics, and the best part is it's free. It allows you to track the visitors on your site, where they came from, how much money they spent if you are running an online store, and you can even track online enquiries if you are running a local business. It's an essential tool for every website.

Call Rail
https://www.callrail.com/

Call Rail is popular for its ease-of-use, international support, integrations with Google Analytics, Google Ads, WordPress, Salesforce and flexibility. It also includes cool features like text messaging, geo-routing, voicemail and more. Plans start at $45 per month.

Call Tracking Metrics
https://www.calltrackingmetrics.com/

Call Tracking Metrics is another popular platform, also offering international support, Google Analytics, Google Ads, WordPress integrations, and overall, similar features to Call Rail. Some online user reports mention preferring Call Rail for its simplicity and flexibility, and found Call Tracking Metrics a little difficult to navigate, but in the end, it's often best to trial both platforms initially and see what works best for your business. Plans start at $39 per month.

Crazy Egg - Free to start. Plants start at $24 per month. https://www.crazyegg.com/

If you want a visual indication of how visitors behave on your site once they arrive, Crazy Egg is a fantastic tool. With Crazy Egg, you can get heat maps of where visitors click on the page. You can also see heat maps of how far visitors scroll down the page.

Google Data Studio
https://datastudio.google.com/overview

Google Data Studio will create visual reports so you can monitor almost anything—calls, ad campaigns on various platforms, search rankings, Salesforce leads, your bookkeeping system, the list goes on. The best part is, it's free.

BONUS CHAPTER: GOOGLE'S ALGORITHM UPDATES.

You need to be informed about Google's updates to ensure your site doesn't trigger Google's spam filters. In some cases, you can take advantage of updates to the algorithm and get higher rankings. In this chapter I will walk you through some of the major recent updates to be aware of. And at the end of this chapter, I will show you resources for catching wind of new updates as they are released. Let's get started.

HTTPS UPDATE & HTTPS UPGRADE CHECKLIST.

In an age of security scandals, mysterious hacking groups, Government surveillance programs—and celebrities sending nude selfies to each other—it's easy to understand why Google, Apple and other tech companies are encouraging everyone to be more secure. Part of this trend is Google's advocacy for website encryption. On August 26th, 2014, Google publicly confirmed they started using SSL security certificates as a ranking signal.

Since Google publicly acknowledged site encryption is a positive ranking factor in its algorithm and stated its intention to strengthen this factor in coming years—it's probably a good idea to install an SSL security certificate on your site.

If that isn't motivation enough, as of October 2017, Google Chrome started showing security warnings to users visiting sites without SSL-enabled. The security notice shows up in Chrome's address bar, stating that the website is "Not Secure", with a strong focus on non-SSL sites containing web forms, and when users visit non-SSL sites in Incognito mode.

If you're wondering what the hell I am talking about, you have probably seen website encryption in action when you log in to your Internet banking or Gmail account. When you see a green padlock at the start of the web address and it has HTTPS at the front, this means the connection is encrypted and the site owner has installed a security certificate and verified ownership of the site.

Website encryption provides a direct connection between the user and the website server, a bit like a tunnel. Because it's encrypted if anybody tries to eavesdrop on this connection any information intercepted will look like gibberish. The only parties who can read the information are the web server and the user. Pretty neat, huh?

Unfortunately, installing a security certificate isn't enough to get an extra boost to your rankings. There is a migration process required to ensure Google picks up everything correctly.

I've listed basic steps below for upgrading your website without any loss in rankings or SEO juice. But this process is more technically involved than weaving a few keywords into the page, you should read the supporting documentation by Google, ask your developer to do this, and maybe even consider using professional SEO help before completing this process.

1. Contact your web host or domain registration provider to install a security certificate. Common fees can range from $50 to $500 per year, depending on the type of certificate.

2. Make sure both HTTPS and HTTP versions of your site continue to run.

3. Upgrade all internal resources and internal links in your HTML code to use relative URLs. This includes references to HTML files, CSS files, Javascript files, images, and all other files referenced in your HTML code. This means instead of referring to internal resources in the website code with an absolute address (e.g. http://www.yourwebsite.com/logo.jpg), it should use a relative address (e.g. ./logo.jpg).

4. Update all of your canonical tags to point to the new HTTPS version of your site.

5. Upload 301 redirects for all HTTP URLs to point to the new HTTPS secured URLs.

6. Verify the new HTTPS version of your site in a new profile in Google Search Console.

7. Upload an XML sitemap to the new HTTPS Google Search Console profile. This sitemap should include all of the old HTTP pages from your site and the new HTTPS pages. We are submitting the old pages to encourage Google to crawl the old pages and register the redirects.

8. Update all links on your social media accounts and other marketing materials to point to the new URLs.

If you want a downloadable copy of this checklist, the SSL upgrade steps for SEO are covered in the free SEO checklist at the end of the book.

Before working through the SSL upgrade steps, make sure you or your developer read through the support guides by Google on performing this upgrade.

Securing your site with HTTPS – Google Search Console Help
https://support.google.com/webmasters/answer/607354 3

Site Moves With URL changes – Google Search Console Help
https://support.google.com/webmasters/answer/603304 9

GOOGLE'S RANKBRAIN & MACHINE LEARNING ANNOUNCEMENT.

In late October 2015, Google announced that its machine-learning artificial-intelligence technology titled RankBrain had been secretly influencing the search results. Does this mean sinister super-intelligent robots created by the genius minds at Google are slowly taking over our search results? Not really.

Over 15% of Google's daily searches have never been searched before. On these never-before-seen types of searches, Google don't have any historic user engagement data to ensure it is delivering the right answer. Understandably, Google needs a strong capability to understand the actual meaning behind a user's search query as they type it into the search box.

Enter RankBrain, RankBrain forms connections between clusters of words to get a better understanding of what a searcher really wants, even if the searcher only gives Google a small amount of information. It then delivers a relevant answer to the searcher's query, even if the results with the best answers don't necessarily use the exact words as the user. RankBrain is also a machine learning technology, which means it progressively learns from analyzing old searches, so it gets better over time.

Google   fastest runner

All   Videos   News   Images   Shopping   More   Settings   Tools

About 34,900,000 results (1.23 seconds)

Usain Bolt

The title of the fastest man of all time goes to **Usain Bolt** (born August 21, 1986), with a time of 9.58 seconds. Mar 21, 2019

Who Are the Top Five Fastest Runners in the World ...
https://howtheyplay.com › olympics › Who-Are-The-Five-Fastest-100-Meter...

In the above example, simply by searching "fastest runner" the first search result lists Usain Bolt at the top of the search results. That's some solid guesswork from Google! We can see Google's strong capability at inferring the actual meaning behind our search, even though I only hinted at the person I am searching about. This is Google's RankBrain technology at work, forming connections behind the scenes. As popular trends come and go, presumably, this matching technology is automatically applied in new searches and organically changes to adapt with the times.

You may be wondering about the impact on professional SEO. The impact is very little. As yet, there have been no disadvantages or advantages reported by SEO professionals, except, it's as important as ever to ensure your page contains related keywords in addition to your targeted keywords. Always ensure Google has enough information as possible to understand the topic of your page, because now it's possible Google will deliver your page for even more search results.

HTTP/2—THE POWERFUL TECHNOLOGY THAT CAN DOUBLE YOUR LOAD SPEED.

The nice folk at Google, Facebook, Firefox and Chrome covertly worked in an underground cave for several years, developing a secret technology that can almost triple the load speed of most web pages. I'm joking about the cave but the technology is very real and now you can use it on your website, too!

HTTP/2 is a technology that significantly improves how servers communicate with web browsers, resulting in dramatic speed increases. On February 11th, 2016 the Google Chrome Developers Blog announced Google Chrome browser's support of this new technology, while deprecating a similar technology called SPDY. SPDY, the older technology for improving browsing speed, was originally created by Google, so for them to decommission SPDY in favor of HTTP/2 might give you an idea of what Google thinks about this new technology...they love it!

If you're not already familiar with HTTP/2, and wondering what I'm rattling on about, HTTP is the technology that all web servers use to transmit files between web servers and web browsers. The old HTTP standard has been used for about 25 years, but being quite old, it wasn't really designed for the high demands of modern web users. The way it sends files is a bit like doing your grocery shopping by purchasing one item individually, packing it in your car, and then returning to the store to purchase the next item, and continuing this way until finished. When you make a request to load a page from the server, your computer needs to open and close a new connection for each file needed to load the page, and can only have a maximum of 6 concurrent connections per web server.

Well HTTP/2 completely revolutionizes the way computers communicate with servers. When your browser contacts the server, the server compresses all the files you need, and sends them over in one tiny little package. The end result is dramatically decreased loading times for all web users, or dramatically increased load speeds—however you want to look at it. Needless to say, with Google's strong ranking advantages associated with fast loading websites, this is a solid technique to have in your SEO toolbox.

Feeling skeptical? Check out the below resource comparing HTTP and HTTP/2 speed differences side-by-side. You might be surprised by the difference.

HTTP/2 Technology Demo
http://www.http2demo.io/

While a great technology, there are a few caveats. Web browsers only widely support HTTP/2 on websites secured with encryption and security certificates, so you'll need one of those to get started.

HTTP/2 is supported by most browsers and web servers, but it can be a little tricky to setup on your web server, and something that should only be performed by a professional web developer or server administrator.

If you want to get started with HTTP/2, the best starting point is to contact your web developer and web hosting company to see if HTTP/2 is supported on your server.

I'm going to make a shout out to the smart guys over at Shopify — would you kindly consider enabling HTTP/2 on your servers? Hundreds of thousands of online retailers are missing out on this load speed advantage, significant sales increases, and millions of shoppers are being delivered slow websites as a result of not having HTTP/2 fully enabled… Apologies for the digression, and I'll get off my high horse now.

Describing how to install HTTP/2 is well beyond the scope of this book, with the infinite amount of web server configurations often requiring different installation methods, but the below resources can be a good starting point for technical information on enabling it on popular web servers, if you're not technically inclined, send them over to your web developer.

How to Enable HTTP/2 in Apache Web Server
https://www.howtoforge.com/how-to-enable-http-2-in-apache/

How to Enable HTTP/2 in Nginx
https://www.howtoforge.com/how-to-enable-http-2-in-nginx/

HTTP/2 Frequently Asked Questions
https://http2.github.io/faq/

GOOGLE'S INTERSTITIAL UPDATE – A.K.A. "DEATH TO MOBILE POPUPS."

In August 2016 Google announced on January 10, 2017 site displaying obtrusive "interstitials" to mobile users wouldn't rank as highly in the search results, and they would banish this type of advertising behavior from the cosmos! If you're wondering what "interstitial" means, it's Silicon Valley tech-speak for a popup ad.

Let's have a quick read over the announcement from the team at Google and then look at what this update means for businesses:

"Here are some examples of techniques that make content less accessible to a user:

- Showing a popup that covers the main content, either immediately after the user navigates to a page from the search results, or while they are looking through the page.
- Displaying a standalone interstitial that the user has to dismiss before accessing the main content.
- Using a layout where the above-the-fold portion of the page appears similar to a standalone interstitial, but the original content has been inlined underneath the fold."

Examples of interstitials that make content less accessible

An example of an   An example of an   Another example of an
intrusive popup   intrusive standalone   intrusive standalone
                          interstitial   interstitial

Examples of interstitials that would not be affected by the new signal, if used responsibly

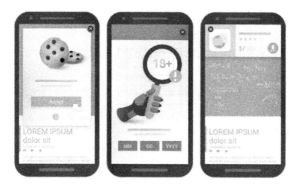

An example of an   An example of an   An example of a banner
interstitial for cookie   interstitial for age   that uses a reasonable
usage   verification   amount of screen
                                                    space

Helping Users Easily Access Content On Mobile
https://webmasters.googleblog.com/2016/08/helping-users-easily-access-content-on.html

In other words, with the exception of cookie verifications and legal notices, age verifications, and app install banners, all other popups will lead to poor performance in the mobile search results.

I'm on the fence on this update, I know from experience a lot of site owners and business owners achieve significant sales from subscribers that sign up to their popups. Dictating the marketing of site owners to such a degree could be considered an over-reach from Google. By making it more difficult for site-owners to maximize the sales of their website visitors, are Google encouraging site owners to spend more money on Google Ads and remarketing campaigns to encourage more customers to return to their site?... I'll let you decide.

On the other hand, a significant number of sites load unnecessarily slow and make mobile web browsing a clunky, slow and unreliable experience. Quite often, the cause of the slow loading is the site owner clogging up their site with complicated scripts and files that power the popup advertisements — sorry, I mean interstitials. Google have played a significant role in nudging website owners to update their technology and make browsing the web an effortless and usable experience, which is good for the Internet community as a whole.

Whatever your feelings about this update, this is going to be a positive change for users. The way we browse the web on our phones will become faster and more reliable as a result. Just ensure you disable mobile pop-ups or you will likely see some drop-offs in your mobile search visitors. Death to popups, long live browser notifications!

ACCELERATED MOBILE PAGES—A.K.A. MOBILE WEB BROWSING ON STEROIDS.

Have you ever asked yourself, "What are Accelerated Mobile Pages all about, exactly?" If you haven't, then maybe you should, because the behemoth open source project known as Accelerated Mobile Pages can help sites get a major boost in the search results. So much so, the Google team announced on September 12, 2016 on the Google Webmaster Central Blog that sites equipped with the Accelerated Mobile Pages technology are going to be rewarded with "expanded exposure." The descriptions are noticeably vague, like most statements from Google, but before jumping to conclusions let's look at what Accelerated Mobile Pages are all about, exactly.

Accelerated Mobile Pages is a collaborative effort between Google, and a gazillion notable publishing companies around the globe, such as Mashable, The Guardian, The New York Times, and many others. The development teams of these organizations have been working together to craft a new technology making mobile web browsing faster, to a significant degree. To their credit, pages enabled with the Accelerated Mobile Pages technology are noticeably fast, snappy and responsive when you view them on your phone.

Specifically, Accelerated Mobile Pages is a framework, or a set of tools and guidelines, enabling web developers to build web pages that load blazingly fast. The core elements of AMP involve a specific approach to coding HTML, a JavaScript library that speeds up the delivery of files, and a caching network provided by Google that ensures speedier delivery of the files.

Some examples of techniques AMP employs to make mobile web browsing super-fast include:

1. Only allowing asynchronous scripts. Quite often websites won't load the page until particular scripts have been downloading in full, with this new restriction it will only accept scripts that load in the background and don't block the loading on the page.

2. Only running GPU-accelerated animations. Believe it or not, some webpages use unreasonably complicated scripts causing your mobile's processor to slow down, with this restriction the AMP creators are forcing simpler calculations on websites that can be processed quickly by the graphics processor on your phone.
3. Pre-rendering, A.K.A. loading pages in advance. Another powerful technique, pre-rending intelligently loads pages you are likely to visit in the background, so that when you get around to visiting them there's no need to wait for it to download.

The above examples are only a few of the many techniques the authors of AMP use to make websites load significantly faster on mobile phones. If you want to check out which platforms support this technology, the folks over at the AMP project have created a list of websites currently providing AMP capability.

Supported Platforms, Vendors & Partners - AMP
https://amp.dev/support/faq/platform-and-vendor-partners/

Getting Started with AMP.

While AMP provides a significant boost in speed and benefits for site owners and their users, to be honest, there is a solid amount of work required to enable it on your site. It's likely AMP may not even fit in with your current design or templates, requiring retooling your website layouts and elements to fit in with AMP's guidelines. The speed boosts are significant, however, so it may be worth considering implementing on your site.

Coding with AMP technology is well beyond the scope of this book, however, the folks over at Google and AMP have put together all-encompassing guides that are updated regularly, making it easier for yourself or your developer to put this technology to work. Have a browse or send the following resources to your developer, and you can get AMP technology running on your site.

Accelerated Mobile Pages– Overview
https://amp.dev/
This home page provides a general overview of AMP, written in a conversational style that should be understandable to both technical and non-technical readers alike.

Accelerated Mobile Pages – How AMP Works
https://amp.dev/about/how-amp-works/

This technical guide provides a more detailed overview of the inner workings of Accelerated Mobile Pages, including tutorials on how to implement it on your website.

Accelerated Mobile Pages GitHub Repository
https://github.com/ampproject/amphtml

For super smart technical types, the AMP Project GitHub Repository has all the updated files and resources needed to get your website running with AMP, as well as all of the source code which is open sourced so you can bask in its transparent wonderfulness.

GOOGLE'S FRED AND PANDA UPDATE—DIAGNOSIS AND RECOVERY.

Around March 8, 2017, murmurs of a Google update echoed around the blogosphere. Prominent Google staff member, Garry Illyes previously joked all future updates should be named "Fred", so the SEO community obliged and labeled this newest update Fred.

While many professionals initially debated the significance and exact focus of the update, industry stalwarts Barry Schwartz from Search Engine Land and Juan Goanzalez from Sistrix put their heads down and analyzed hundreds of sites that lost massive amounts of traffic, up to 90% in some cases, and they found something interesting. Sites affected were guilty of a surprisingly small set of possible infringements, two in fact, which could be witnessed on affected sites. The common attributes were largely on-page and quality focused, making this update likely focused on improving the Google Panda part of the algorithm — which deals with assessing page quality.

Common Attributes of FRED Affected Sites.

1) Sites affected showed a strong commercial focus over providing real value for users. This means sites with large amounts of pages filled with low quality content in an effort to generate ad revenue.

2) Sites affected generally feature aggressive ad placements, taking up a large amount of screen real estate "above-the-fold" or hidden in the content in a way that confuses users.

Google FRED Recovery Steps.

The update is clearly focused on content quality, much like previous Panda updates, thus the solution is fairly straight forward for victims of this update — improve your content and take it easy on the ads. In many cases, site owners hit by the update made a complete recovery simply by dialing down their ad placements above the fold. If you think you were hit by this update, take a look at the following recovery steps. As with all updates, you should only complete the following steps if you are confident you were definitely affected by the penalty.

1. Look over your rankings and traffic around the 8th of March, 2017. If you experienced a drop off in both rankings and traffic on this day, and the drop off is significant (i.e. it looks like your rankings and traffic fell off a cliff) then it's likely you've been hit by Google FRED.
2. Next look at your content and advertisement strategy on your site. Does your website create a lot of low quality articles to drive ad revenue, or does it feature aggressive ad placements to drive ad revenue? If you're guilty of either of these, and you saw the clear drop off in traffic then it's almost certain you've been hit by FRED.
3. If you're guilty of aggressive ad placement above the fold, you want to try modifying your ad placement strategy. This includes reducing your amount of above the fold ads, and also spacing out your ads so they are not deceptively mixed in with content.

4. If you're guilty of having large numbers of low quality pages, you either want to improve the content or take low quality pages down. Improving content is the better option, if you make a recovery you will recover more traffic than deleting offending pages.

5. When finished, update your sitemap and resubmit to Google in Google Search Console. This step will encourage Googlebot to visit your website and pick up the changes.

6. Monitor Google Analytics and any rankings tracking software you use. Rinse and repeat if necessary.

GOOGLE'S LOCAL SEO HAWK & POSSUM UPDATES.

On August 22, 2017, local SEO industry analyst Joy Hawkins, founder of Sterling Sky consulting, and occasional contributor to Search Engine Land, broke news of a significant update to the local SEO algorithm, subsequently dubbed the "Hawk" update.

She discovered that Google rolled back, or at least fixed, some of the changes to the Possum local SEO update that shook up the local SEO results way back in September 2016.

The previous Possum update had some bugs that would inadvertently filter out individual businesses in close proximity to each other. For example, if your businesses occupied the same building with a competitor in the same industry, or even down the same street, you could potentially completely fall off the local rankings—if your competitor had stronger local signals than you.

After the Hawk update, Google loosened their proximity filter up a little bit, so local businesses within close proximity, unfairly affected by the Possum update, are given a fairer chance in the results.

Businesses still affected by the Possum update, or the "close proximity filter" Google use in their local algorithm, includes businesses in the same industry using the same "virtual addresses", businesses in the same industry occupying the same building, and even businesses in different buildings up to 50 feet away from their competitor—now still often filtered out from the local search results.

So, if you're looking at opening up a new business, better make sure you don't choose the same building (or virtual address) as your competitor, or you might find yourself fighting an impossible battle trying to work your way into the local search results.

GOOGLE BECOMING APPLE'S DEFAULT SEARCH PROVIDER FOR SIRI, IOS AND SPOTLIGHT ON MAC OS.

On September 25, 2017, Apple announced they made the switch from Bing to Google as their default search provider for Siri, iOS search, and Spotlight search on Mac OS—a big news event in 2017 for everyone living in search engine universe.

The reason for the switch, stated by Apple, was Apple wants users to have a consistent search experience for users across all their apps and devices.... Google's state-of-the-art search technology likely took part in this decision... And, possibly, just a guess, the $9 billion annual contract Google is now paying Apple to remain Apple's default search provider on iOS devices—I'll let you form your own opinion on whatever the final deciding factor was, but moving on...

Part of the agreement requires all searches through Apple to be encrypted and anonymized, to ensure Apple's enduring stance on safeguarding privacy for users. Good news for Apple users.

You might be wondering what this means for the average user or business? Well first up, with close to a billion iPhones in active circulation worldwide—it's certainly going to lead to more traffic and customers for businesses performing well in the Google search results.

Secondly, well, we're not really sure what the other impacts may be. With increasing voice search popularity, including Siri, it might become more important for business owners to ensure their business names are easy to pronounce...

So, if you were thinking of naming your new Indian restaurant "Patek's Delicious and Delectable Culinary Indian Delights" you might want to make your business name something more pronounceable, like "Patek's Indian Restaurant Los Angeles", and make it a little bit easier on Siri... Poor Siri...

Either way, it's blue skies from here for site owners performing well in the Google search results — more users means more customers and more sales.

GOOGLE'S GAME-CHANGING MOBILE-FIRST INDEX.

After much anticipation and speculation by the SEO community — Google officially announced the live rollout of their Mobile First Index on the 26th of March, 2018. Let's look at official wording from Google's 'Best Practices for Mobile-First Indexing' guide...

"Mobile-first indexing means Google will predominantly use the mobile version of the content for indexing and ranking.

Historically, the index primarily used the desktop version of a page's content when evaluating the relevance of a page to a user's query. Since the majority of users now access Google via a mobile device, the index will primarily use the mobile version of a page's content going forward. We aren't creating a separate mobile-first index. We continue to use only one index."

Want simple language? Google is now using the mobile version of websites as the first touchpoint in calculating the search index and search results, for both desktop and mobile results... Hold up a minute... Did I just say that the mobile version site will be the FIRST touchpoint for calculating BOTH results... Damn straight!

Makes sense when you think about it. The vast majority of the Internet are mobile users. To ensure smartphone addicts are delivered with better results on the move, it makes sense for Google to make mobile the highest priority in the algorithm, with desktop quickly becoming a small minority of Internet users.

Outcomes and action steps for site owners.

If you haven't jumped on the mobile bandwagon by now — with mobile traffic making up around 70%-80% of traffic for most sites — you're missing out on traffic right this very second and it's possible you will eventually completely fall off the mobile results.

Fortunately, there's an elegant solution discussed earlier in the mobile SEO section in the on-page SEO chapter, but I'll let Google spokesperson Gary Illyes take the reins, with a direct quote from a discussion about the update at the SMX Advanced search conference in Seattle...

"If you have a responsive site, then you're pretty much good to go. Why? Because the content on your desktop site will be pretty much the same on your responsive site. The structured data on your desktop site will be the same."

In other words, if your site is responsive and supporting mobile users, you can lie back and enjoy a Piña Colada, knowing your desktop-only competitors will eventually fall to the wayside, while you bask in the glory of a mobile-first paradise for users.

For the detail-a-holics out there, here are the likely scenarios for varying mobile implementations...

- Desktop sites with no mobile versions will not be crawled by Google's special mobile spider called 'Smartphone Googlebot.' They will continue to be crawled by desktop Google and likely perform worse in mobile results due to Google's continued focus on improving mobile results for mobile users.
- Sites with responsive web designs (supporting both desktop and mobile in the one design) will continue to perform the same in both desktop and mobile results.
- Sites built entirely in AMP HTML will continue to perform the same in both desktop and mobile results.
- Sites using separate URLs for mobile visitors will have the mobile URLs crawled by the smartphone spider and rankings adjusted accordingly.
- Sites dynamically serving different content for desktop and mobile users will have the mobile content crawled and rankings adjusted accordingly.
- Sites using both AMP and non-AMP versions of pages will have the non-AMP mobile version of the page crawled by Googlebot and rankings adjusted accordingly.

Summing it up — not much to do really, besides making sure your mobile support is top notch. If you need to improve your mobile support, read the mobile support section in the on-page SEO chapter. And if you want to read about all the bells and whistles involved with this particular update, Google have put together a digestible guide for business owners and developers alike, available below...

Best Practices for Mobile First Indexing - Google
https://developers.google.com/search/mobile-sites/mobile-first-indexing

GOOGLE'S MOBILE "SPEED UPDATE".

Smartphone users want answers delivered fast—as discovered in a study conducted by Google in February, 2018 titled "New Industry Benchmarks for Mobile Page Speed." The study analyzed site speed impacts on mobile users, uncovering interesting but not entirely surprising insights...

- When mobile load times increase from 1s to 10s, the probability of users leaving your site increases by 123%.
- When the number of page elements increases from 400 to 7000—titles, text, images, and so on—conversion probability drops by 95%.... In other words, thrown everything but the kitchen sink into your page? You're only achieving half of your potential sales.

It comes with little surprise in January, 2018 Google announced an upcoming update titled the "Speed Update," rolling out July 2018. Google are tight-lipped about updates, so when they make an announcement, it's something business owners and developers must prioritize.

Site speed was previously used for desktop results. Google's Speed Update will focus on mobile results. Google didn't reveal exact impacts to the slow loading sites — but it's safe to say, slow sites won't be rewarded with higher mobile rankings...

Wondering what to do? Simple. Make your site load fast on mobile. Your rankings will be safe and sales will likely go up too. Instructions for improving load speed are covered in the load speed section in the on-page SEO chapter, for both desktop and mobile speed improvements. The following resources cover this update and include resources specifically focused on improving mobile load speed.

Using Page Speed in Mobile Search Ranking - Google
https://webmasters.googleblog.com/2018/01/using-page-speed-in-mobile-search.html

Test Your Mobile Website Speed and Performance - Google
https://www.thinkwithgoogle.com/feature/testmysite/

Find Out How You Stack Up to New Industry Benchmarks for Mobile Page Speed
https://www.thinkwithgoogle.com/marketing-resources/data-measurement/mobile-page-speed-new-industry-benchmarks/

GOOGLE'S "MEDIC UPDATE"—A.K.A "YOUR MONEY OR YOUR LIFE."

On the 1st of August, 2018 shockwaves echoed across the SEO stratosphere. Google released an update shaking up the results, with sites showing up to 50% gains and 50% losses in Internet traffic. Google released a tight-lipped comment on Twitter...

"Last week, we released a broad core algorithm update. We do these routinely several times per year.... There's no 'fix' for pages that may perform less well other than to remain focused on building great content. Over time, it may be that your content may rise relative to other pages."

That's some vague advice... Fortunately, several industry SEO analysts did intense research revealing sites affected and why. The venerable Barry Schwartz, of Search Engine Land fame, coined this "The Medic Update", with the medical industry suffering the biggest impact. But this title is misleading, impacted sites include any site or page affecting financial or physical well-being of users... So, I hereby call it, the "Your Money or Your Life Update", as it affects both the money and life of users—and ultimately, the financial well-being of website owners... Let's look at the YMYL update's common attributes.

YMYL update common attributes.

- Impacted sites and pages cover topics that affect Internet users' physical and financial well-being.
- Impacted sites saw up to 10%-50% decreases or increases in search engine traffic around the 1st of August 2018.
- YMYL sites with low trust saw decreased rankings.
- YMYL sites with high trust saw increased rankings.
- The update also affected low quality YMYL sites, such as aggressive popups and auto-play ads.
- The trust and quality factors observed in affected sites are published in Google's Search Quality Evaluator Guidelines. Examples include making site ownership clear on an about page, reputable authors posting on sensitive topics, quality content, not having annoying popups and ads, and so on. Google's Search Quality whitepaper location is included later in this section.

Action steps if negatively affected by the YMYL update.

Like all updates, it's always a solid move to get a second opinion, ensuring you're not fixing problems that don't need to be fixed and unnecessarily damage your site. That said, follow these steps if possibly affected by the update.

1. Using Google Analytics, review search traffic around the 1st of August, 2018. And review search visibility in Google Search Console. If you see a sharp drop-off in search traffic and visibility, more than 10% or 15%, it's possible you've been affected by the update.
2. If your site generates ad revenue and revenue dropped off, don't go crazy filling your site up with extra ads. It will make things worse.

3. Review your site to see if it is guilty of the YMYL update common attributes listed earlier.

4. Re-read Google's Search Quality Guidelines covered in the On Page SEO chapter in this book. Google's trust and quality factors are covered there, listing causes and remedies for site owners suffering from the YMYL update.

5. Get to work improving these areas. You should see gradual improvements over several weeks.

6. The above steps should cover 99% of cases. If you clearly lost traffic around the 1st of August, 2018, and don't see any progress after the above action steps, you might have to read Google's Search Quality Evaluator Guidelines to improve traffic. Yes, it's 160-pages long. Yes, if I had to choose between reading a 160-page document and losing more traffic and sales, I'd read the document.

Google Search Quality Evaluator Guidelines – May, 2019
https://static.googleusercontent.com/media/guidelines.r aterhub.com/en//searchqualityevaluatorguidelines.pdf

GOOGLE'S NEW NOFOLLOW LINK GUIDELINES FOR 2020.

Ever heard of the rel="nofollow" tag on links? It was introduced by Google way back in 2005, to help Google detect and filter out sponsored, paid or spammy links. The tag is also used for site-owners to openly tell Google links are paid, preventing site-owners from getting into Google's naughty book for selling links on the down-low for shady purposes.

Fast forward to September 2019, and now Google wants more information about the links on your site, introducing three new types of rel tags, which they'll use as a hint to calculate the rankings. Here's the three new types of rel tags introduced by Google...

rel="sponsored" - links that are advertisements or paid placements.
rel="ugc"- user-generated content (UGC) links, such as comments and forum posts, as ugc.
rel="nofollow" - use when other values don't apply, when you'd rather Google not associate your site with the outgoing link, or crawl the link from your site.

Wondering what to do about this update? Google made it clear in their announcement to not go back and change all the old nofollow links on your site — and I agree. Going through and changing all old nofollow links on your site could have unpredictable consequences, unless you really know what you are doing.

Moving forward, simply add the above tags to new links added to your site starting from... Now. You can add multiple rel attributes to links, where relevant, by separating them with a space. Official guidelines from Google listed below.

Qualify Your Outbound Links to Google - Google Search Console Help
https://support.google.com/webmasters/answer/96569

GOOGLE'S BERT UPDATE—GOOGLE FINALLY LEARNS HOW HUMANS SPEAK.

Google   movie 1980s people experiment dying kiefer sutherland

All   News   Images   Videos   Shopping   More   Settings   Tools

About 246,000 results (1.22 seconds)

Flatliners

Flatliners is a 1990 American science fiction psychological horror film directed by Joel Schumacher, produced by Michael Douglas and Rick Bieber, and written by Peter Filardi. It stars Kiefer Sutherland, Julia Roberts, William Baldwin, Oliver Platt, and Kevin Bacon.

Flatliners - Wikipedia
https://en.wikipedia.org › wiki › Flatliners

Let's face it—we're getting lazy about how we use the Internet... Getting out the laptop feels like a drag, we're shouting shorthand voice searches into our phones like, "movie 1990s people experiment dying kiefer sutherland", expecting Google to do the heavy lifting...

And it does—displaying the Wikipedia entry for 1990's film "Flatliners", a cult-classic about medical students experimenting with near-death-experiences. On the Flatliners Wikipedia page, the word "experiment" appears only once, but Kiefer Sutherland appeared in over 29 movies in the 1990s in which lots of characters died. Notice how I accidentally typed in 1980s and Google figured it out, anyway? Solid work by Google.

To combat increasing ambiguity in searches, 15 percent of searches being entirely brand new — and just get a better grasp on human language — on October 21st, 2019 Google announced their biggest leap forward in search technology since RankBrain called... BERT.

Or for-short, Bidirectional Encoder Representations from Transformers... A machine-learning technology to better understand human language.

In Google's big BERT announcement, the VP of Search described how Google would previously struggle with searches like "can you get medicine for someone pharmacy", delivering a non-specific result about getting prescriptions filled.

After BERT, Google understands the searcher's intent better, now delivering a result about whether a patient can send a friend or family member to get their prescription filled.

Quick take-aways about this groundbreaking update by Google:

- BERT is expected to impact up to 10% of searches.
- BERT is entirely focused on better understanding the way humans actually communicate (a type of machine learning called Natural Language Processing).
- Searches affected include queries with Homonyms and Polysemes (e.g. the verb "run" is a Polyseme, with 606 different-but-similar meanings according to the Oxford Dictionary).
- Other searches affected include conversational or shorthand queries — such as "parking on a hill with no curb." The last part of this search transforms the intent of the search. This is where the "Bidirectional" aspect of BERT's algorithm comes into play.
- Top-performing sites didn't report any major losses or gains in traffic and rankings after the update.
- Pages targeting long-tail searches will most likely benefit from this update.

Like all algorithm updates, SEO professionals industry-wide analyzed the update upside-down and back-to-front to find an edge… And the general consensus is — not much to do, besides following regular best-practices, making sure your page shows high quality content, including related keywords, LSI keywords and natural language on your pages... And perhaps targeting more long-tail keywords. If you want to read up on the update in greater detail, check out Google's announcement below.

Understanding Searches Better Than Ever Before – Google Blog
https://blog.google/products/search/search-language-understanding-bert

KEEPING UP-TO-DATE WITH GOOGLE'S UPDATES.

As of the last couple of years, Google updates have become progressively frequent. While I understand the constant changes by Google might make you feel like banging your head against the wall and doing a nudie run through the office, don't be disheartened. It can be easy to keep up and the resources below are great for staying updated. If there's a significant update to Google's algorithm, it will be covered on at least one of the following pages.

Google Algorithm Change History
https://moz.com/google-algorithm-change

Google Webmaster Central Blog
https://webmasters.googleblog.com/

Google PageRank & Algorithm Updates
https://www.seroundtable.com/category/google-updates

GOOGLE'S 2020 UPDATES—WHAT'S ON THE HORIZON?

You don't need a crystal ball or secret informer at Google to get a general sense of what's on the horizon. After reviewing decades of updates made to Google's search algorithm, or just previous months, it's easy to get a general idea of what changes Google is likely to make.

Before looking at what's coming up, let's look at what previous Google updates have in common. Almost all previous updates can give us insights into upcoming updates. Previous updates generally focus on two things; 1) filtering out spam and low-quality websites, and 2) making the Internet and Google a better user experience. To figure out what Google may be working on, we should look at possible improvements with these qualities, and also updates Google have publicly acknowledged as being on their agenda.

1. Voice search continues to rise.

Comscore predicted half of all searches will be voice-based by the end of 2020. This is hardly a surprise with the dominance of mobile as the primary Internet platform and the increasing popularity of voice assistants. Voice search will continue to be a key area of focus for Google, and forward-thinking marketers and business owners getting ahead on this trend will be rewarded with increased traffic.

2. Video becomes essential for every marketer and business owner.

Video is huge. So huge, it's predicted to be 80% of Internet by 2021 by Cisco. According to a 2018 study by Sparktoro, YouTube is the second largest search engine – that's right, the second largest. As YouTube and online video's popularity grows, it becomes a powerful yet underused marketing channel for business owners. Likely, eventually an essential marketing channel – because users are addicted to watching cat videos and other things while laying in bed playing with their phones.

3. Rich snippets and structured data becomes required knowledge for every SEO professional.

Google's search results have moved away from the traditional list of links layout, now featuring a diverse mix of results including featured snippets, Q&A results, images, videos and more. Learning structured data and how to achieve rich result rankings will become essential knowledge for anyone taking SEO seriously.

4. The rise of the machine learning algorithms.

Google released their first machine learning algorithm on user behavior, RankBrain, in 2015. Google released their second machine learning algorithm focused on better understanding search queries, BERT, in 2019. With Google's management being very vocal about A.I. as a top priority, Google will continue working machine learning tech in their algorithms. It's hard to know for-sure, the next major machine learning release could potentially focus on better assessing a page's authority and popularity, with a focus on backlinks and social media signals.

That covers probable areas of focus for Google over the next 12 months, based on current trends, and what many industry insiders believe are areas of focus for Google.

I am not a psychic and I cannot see into the future — the above are just educated guesses. Don't run out and change your whole business based on speculation. That said, keep these areas in the back of your mind, so you don't get caught with your pants down from a Google update.

Focus on improving the quality and trust of your site, provide good mobile support, earn relevant backlinks, focus on structured data and rich snippets, and improve the user behavior on your site. If you focus on these areas it's unlikely you will run into any major problems, and you will increase your online performance at the same time.

BONUS CHAPTER 2: THE QUICK AND DIRTY GUIDE TO PAY-PER-CLICK ADVERTISING WITH GOOGLE ADS.

WHY BOTHER WITH PAY-PER-CLICK ADVERTISING?

You would have to be as crazy as a box of weasels to pay each time someone visits your site with pay-per-click advertising, when you can rank high in Google for free, right?

Not necessarily. Pay-per-click advertising has some advantages over SEO, with PPC campaigns you can:

- Send customers to your site within hours, not the months it sometimes takes for solid SEO results.
- Track results down to the penny, and get very clear insights into the financial performance of your advertising. Simply set up conversion tracking with the instructions provided by Google, or whichever pay-per-click provider you choose.
- Achieve a much larger overall number of customers to your site by running pay-per-click in tandem with your other marketing efforts.
- In most cases, achieve a positive financial return on your marketing spend and keep on selling to these customers in the future.

There is one caveat to the last point. If you are a small fish trying to enter an extremely competitive market, such as house loans, insurance or international plane flights, it's likely the big players in the market are buying a large amount of advertising, forcing the average cost-per-click to astronomical prices, and making it difficult for new players to get a profitable return.

If you're selling pizza delivery in New York, pool cleaning in Los Angeles, or cheap baseball jackets... In other words, if you're selling a common local trade, service, or product online, it's likely you can receive a profitable return on your advertising spend.

While pay-per-click marketing really deserves its own book, this is a quick and dirty bonus chapter, jam-packed with just enough information to get a pay-per-click campaign setup, avoid common mistakes, and send more customers and sales to your business.

If you want to delve deeper into the science of pay-per-click advertising, I've included some great resources on Google Ads at the end of the chapter. Sound good? Let's get started.

WHICH IS THE BEST PPC PROVIDER TO START WITH?

There are many pay-per-click providers out there, Google Ads and Bing Ads are just two.

Google Ads text ads is generally the best starting point. You can sell anything on Google Ads if you have money to spend because the user base is so large.

If you're looking to jump into pay-per-click advertising, get started with Google Ads. Move on to the other pay-per-click networks after you have some experience under your belt.

Here's why I think Google Ads text ads is usually the best choice for a first venture into pay-per-click advertising:

- With Google's search engine market share at 88.61%, and Bing at 2.72%, you can reach out to the largest potential amount of customers with Google.
- Fast and instant results. Send new customers to your site within a couple of hours.
- Advanced targeting technology. Target users based on where they are located, or what browser or device they are using. Google's ad targeting technology is among the best in the world.
- Due to the popularity of Google Ads, there's a wealth of knowledge on running Google Ads campaigns successfully.

ENSURING SUCCESS WITH RESEARCH AND A PLAN.

Like all marketing projects, for a Google Ads campaign to be successful, you need to start with research and a solid plan. Without first defining your goals, and designing a robust strategy to achieve them, it's impossible to create a successful marketing campaign — you'll have no way of determining if the outcome is successful!

Here are some important questions to ask yourself before you get started:

- What is the objective of the campaign? Sales, web inquiries, sign-ups, or branding?
- What is the maximum monthly budget you can afford?
- What is the maximum cost-per-inquiry, or cost-per-sale you can afford? For example, if you are selling snow jackets at $100, and your profit margin is 20%, you really can't afford to spend much more than $20 on each customer you acquire. Write this figure down and review it later. You may need to first run a small test campaign to determine if pay-per-click is profitable, and the right tool for marketing your business.
- What are the most common characteristics of your customers? For example, if you're selling late-night pizza delivery in New York, you don't want to be paying for the lovely folk in Idaho searching for late-night pizza delivery. Write down your customers' common characteristics, and later in the settings recommendations, if there's an option to target these customers, I'll tell you how to target them.

HOW TO CHOOSE THE RIGHT KIND OF KEYWORDS.

It's the moment you've been waiting for. The keywords! Precious keywords.

Just like SEO, getting your keywords right with text ads is critical if you want a successful campaign.

Unlike SEO, with Google's text ads there are different types of keywords called keyword match-types. I've listed the main keyword match types below.

Broad match keywords.

The default type of keywords all Google Ads campaign use — if you don't change any settings — are broad match keywords. With broad match keywords, Google will take any word out of your phrase, and serve up ads for searches hardly related to your phrase.

Needless to say, almost all new campaigns should NOT be using broad match keywords to start with. Have a look at the example below.

keyword:
tennis shoes

will trigger ads for:
designer shoes
dress shoes
basketball shoes
tennis bags

tennis equipment

Phrase match keywords.

Phrase match keywords will only show your ad for searches containing your core phrase. With phrase match keywords, you can exercise a higher level of control and purchase traffic from more relevant customers. And higher relevancy usually means more sales.

To enter a phrase match keyword, when adding keywords to your account, wrap the keywords with "" quotation marks and these keywords will become broad match keywords.

keyword:
"tennis shoes"

will trigger ads for:
tennis shoes
best tennis shoes
tennis shoes online

will not trigger ads for:
shoes tennis
tennis shoe
tennis sneakers
tennis players

Exact match keywords.

Exact match keywords will only trigger ads for the exact phrase you enter, and close variants. Needless to say, with exact match keywords in your campaign, you can have a high level of accuracy, and achieve more sales. Exact match keywords are indispensable for every Google Ads campaign.

To enter exact match keywords, wrap the keywords with [] brackets when adding keywords to your account, they will become exact match keywords.

keyword:
[tennis shoes]

will trigger ads for:
tennis shoes
tennis shoe

will not match for:
tennis shoes online
best tennis shoes

Broad match modified keywords.

Broad match modified keywords are special keywords allowing you to have both accuracy and a large amount of exposure. With broad match modified keywords, you will trigger ads that include a combination of all of the words in your phrase.

To create broad match modified keywords, add a + sign to the keywords when adding them to your account.

keyword:
+tennis +shoes

will match for:
where to buy tennis shoes online
tennis shoes
buy shoes for tennis
buy tennis shoes

will not match for:
tennis joggers
buy tennis shoe
margaret thatcher

Negative keywords.

One of the most important, but easily overlooked keywords are negative keywords. Negative keywords will prevent your ads from showing for searches that include your negative keyword.

If you are using phrase match or any kind of broad match keyword, you should be using negative keywords. Negative keywords are vital for ensuring you are not paying for advertising for irrelevant searches.

Enter negative keywords in your campaign by adding a - minus sign in front of your keywords when adding keywords, or going to the shared library on the left hand column in your Google Ads account, and you can apply negative keywords across your entire account, a great time-saving tip.

keywords:
+car +service
-guide
-manual

will trigger ads for:
car service los angeles
car service mechanic
car service tips

will not trigger ads for:
free car service guide
ford mustang 65 car service manual

When choosing keywords, you need a balance between keywords with a high level of accuracy, such as exact match keywords, and keywords with a larger amount of reach, such as phrase match or broad match modified keywords.

Use a mix of the above keywords in your campaign, then review the performance of different keyword types after your campaign has been running, when you have some data.

STRUCTURING YOUR CAMPAIGN WITH AD GROUPS.

Google Ads offers an excellent way of organizing keywords called ad groups.

If you organize your campaign correctly with ad groups, you can quickly see which areas of your campaign are profitable and not so profitable.

Let's say you have a Harley Davidson dealership, with a wide range of HD gear from bikes to accessories and clothing, below is an example of ad groups you might create.

- Harley Davidson motorbikes
- Harley Davidson parts
- Harley Davidson accessories
- Harley Davidson jackets

With ad groups you can:

- Create multiple, and separate ads for each product line. Great for testing.
- Have a select range of keywords, specific to the ad group.
- Set a specific bid for the ad group. Great if you have higher-priced products or services you're willing to pay more for.
- Get detailed data on the performance of your ad groups and different products.

Structure your campaign with ad groups with a very clear and simple sense of organization when you setup your campaign. You'll get clearer performance insights, and it will make your life easier when you want to make improvements later on down the track.

HOW TO CRUSH THE COMPETITION WITH KILLER TEXT ADS.

Writing a killer text ad is essential to the success of your campaign. Poorly written ads can increase the overall costs of your campaign, sending less traffic to your site for more money. We don't want that.

With your text ads, you want to:

- Attract clicks from interested customers, not tire-kickers.
- Include keywords related to what the user searched for.
- Encourage a clear call to action and benefit for the user.

Google   flowers online   🎤 🔍

🔍 All   🛒 Shopping   📖 Books   🖼 Images   📰 News   ⋮ More   Settings   Tools

About 3,100,000,000 results (0.71 seconds)

1-800-FLOWERS.COM® | Same Day Delivery Available
[Ad] www.1800flowers.com/flower/delivery ▾ (855) 318-4890
Whatever the occasion, count on 1-800-Flowers® to deliver smiles. Shop flowers & gifts. Get Same Day Delivery on Our Wide Selection of Flowers And Gifts. Shop 1800FLOWERS®!

Deal of The Week   Birthday Flowers & Gifts
Check Out All of This Weeks Great   Bouquets & Gifts at 1-800 Flowers!
Flower Deals. Don't Miss Out.   Send Your Best Birthday Wishes.

Text ads are made up of the following components:

1. Headline. Your headline has a maximum of 25 characters. With your headline, you should include the keyword the user is searching for or capture the user's curiosity.

2. Description lines. You have two description lines at a maximum of 35 characters each. Your description lines should make it crystal clear what you are selling, the benefits of clicking through to your site and a call-to-action.

3. Display URL. You have 35 characters for a custom URL that will be displayed to users in the search results. Display URLs are great as you can actually display a different URL to the users than the URL of the page they will arrive on. You can take advantage of this to encourage more users to arrive on your site.

I've listed below some winning ads so we can see why they are so successful:

Logo Design ® *SALE* $49
www.logodesignguarantee.com/Logo-USA
100% Custom-Made Special USA Sale
100% Money Back. Order Online Now…

Injured in an Accident?
www.1800needhelp.com/
You May Be Entitled to $10,000 +
Free Case Evaluation. 24/7 Call Us

Flowers Online - $19.99
www.fromyouflowers.com/
Delivered Today Beautiful & Fresh!
"Best Value Flowers" - CBS News

In each of the above, we can see some similarities. Each ad has:

- An interesting headline. Each ad captures the curiosity of the user, through use of special characters, asking a question or posting a competitive offer right in the headline.
- Clear benefits. Each ad has a compelling offer in addition to the core product or service being sold, making the ad stand out from the search results, such as a no-risk, money-back guarantee, same-day delivery, or a free evaluation.
- A clear call-to-action. The first two ads make it clear what the next step should be. In the third ad, the call-to-action is not explicit, but it is obvious. By having "Online - $19.99" in the headline, and "Delivered Today", it is clear the user can order flowers online to be delivered the same-day.

If you want more examples of successful text ads and why they crush the competition, the article below is a good starting point:

11 successful ads and why they crush the competition
https://www.crazyegg.com/blog/successful-adwords-ads/

HOW MUCH TO PAY FOR KEYWORDS.

A burning question for text ads newbies is, how much should I bid on my keywords?

There is no clear answer for finding your ideal bid price. You should only pay for what you can afford. You can find out how much you can afford by doing some simple math.

For example, let's look at an example scenario:

- You're selling video courses for $200.
- For every 100 visitors, 3 turn into customers. This is a conversion rate of 3%.
- If you bought 100 visitors at a cost-per-click of $3, this would cost $300.
- With your 3% conversion rate, you will have made $600 in sales, and a profit of $300

So to calculate your ideal CPC, I'm sorry to say, you do need to sit down and do some math and figure it out. It cannot be avoided. But to keep it simple, you should only pay what you can afford — otherwise you should be spending your marketing dollars elsewhere.

Here's the catch, you can only find out what your cost-per-click is after running your campaign for a while, when you have accumulated some data. So, run a small test campaign to begin with, to collect data. Use the information to make projections, and only pay what you can afford in a larger, more serious campaign.

In case you're wondering how prices get calculated, the Google Ads cost-per-click network uses a bidding system, which means you are taking place in an auction with competing advertisers. By increasing bids, your ad position increases, leading to more traffic or customers to your site.

Here is where it gets interesting. Google awards an advantage to advertisers showing ads with high quality and high relevancy. This is Google's Quality Score technology. Ads with a higher number of clicks and relevancy are awarded with a higher Quality Score, and subsequently receive increased ad positions and cheaper prices!

Keep this in mind when writing ads and choosing your keywords. Your ads should be relevant to achieve the highest Quality Score possible, so you can receive the cheapest cost-per-click.

GOOGLE ADS SETTINGS FOR GETTING STARTED.

The single most important factor to ensure your campaign is successful is to fill out all of the settings when you set up your campaign. Whatever you do, do not rush through the campaign settings, otherwise you will end up paying for advertising to people who have no interest in what you're selling.

I've listed recommended Google Ads settings below for reference, but if you are not setting up your Google Ads campaign right now, feel free to skip to the end of this chapter for closing recommendations on reviewing Google Ads campaigns for long-term success.

1. If you haven't done so already, create an account at https://ads.google.com/home/. When signing up, enter your Google account, or let the tool create one for you if you don't already have one.

2. Once fully signed in, click on the big button "Create your first campaign."

3. Campaign name:
Enter a descriptive name for your campaign.

4. Type:
Choose "search network only" from the drop-down. This is important. Make sure you select this option, unless you know what you are doing, otherwise you will also end up buying advertising on less relevant sites.

Select "All features - All options for the Search Network, with Display Select." Why would we want to restrict ourselves and give ourselves less options and features? Choose it, features are awesome. Trust me.

5. Networks:
Unselect "include search partners." We want to advertise on Google, not other smaller, potentially less-relevant sites.

6. Locations:
If you are targeting customers from a specific area, country, state or city, enter the most relevant setting for your customers here. Whatever you do, don't forget about this setting, otherwise if you're a local business you'll end up buying advertising halfway around the world!

7. Bid strategy:
Choose "I'll manually set my bids for clicks." This allows you to make sure you are only setting cost-per-click bids you can afford. More on setting bids later.

8. Default bid:
Enter any number here, we are going to change it later.

9. Budget:
Enter your daily budget.

10. Ad Extensions:
Ad Extensions, otherwise known as sitelinks, are a great way to encourage more clicks to your site. Enter as many relevant entries as you can, if you have an office address and phone number, use it.

11. Schedule:
If you are only open during certain business hours, enter the hours you want to be running ads here. For some businesses, it's OK to run your campaign 24/7, because some customers will send an online inquiry if they arrive at your site outside of business hours. If you are selling something like a local food, such as a pizza shop, you might want to restrict your campaigns to only run during your opening hours.

12. Ad delivery:
Choose "Rotate indefinitely. Show lower performing ads more evenly with higher performing ads, and do not optimize."

Why would you want to choose this, you might wonder? You want to run your ads evenly, so you have reliable data when you review your ads, and can objectively see which ads are performing better for your goals.

You can leave the rest of settings for now, hit "save and continue", and you're good to go with setting up the rest of your campaign.

OPTIMIZATION TIPS FOR TWEAKING YOUR CAMPAIGN FOR BETTER PROFIT.

I've touched on a handful of secrets of successful pay-per-click campaigns, but I'm going to cover the most important technique for pay-per-click success.

Review your campaign regularly.

Leaving a Google Ads campaign running without keeping your head around the performance is like leaving a freight train running without a driver.

Regularly review your ad, ad group, keyword, cost-per-click, and cost-per-conversion performance. This will allow you to back the winning horses of your campaign, and swiftly cut the losers.

Fortunately, the Google Ads platform offers endless opportunities for deep insights into the performance of your campaign.

As a starting point, below are example areas in your campaign to regularly look over:

- Ad group performance. Review click-through-rates, cost-per-click, and cost-per-conversion. Allocate more funds from your campaign to winning ad groups, and decrease funds or pause losing ad groups if you see any obvious trends.
- Ad performance. Look for winning ads with higher click-through-rates, lower cost-per-clicks, and lower cost-per-conversion. Pause expensive ads, and create new ads to split-test based on your winners. Progressively build up new ads with higher click-through-rates into your campaign over time.
- Keyword performance. Review which keywords are running at a higher cost, which keywords have low quality scores, and see if you can pause any overly budget-draining keywords with low conversions.

USING ACCELERATED MOBILE PAGES IN GOOGLE ADS CAMPAIGNS TO ACCELERATE YOUR SALES.

Late September 2017, Google rolled out Accelerated Mobile Pages (AMP) support for Google Ads campaigns. Why is this important? AMP significantly increases load speed for mobile users. Faster load times equals higher conversion rates, and higher conversion rates means more sales. In fact, the smart lads over at Google's AMP team reported increases up to 80% in mobile conversion rates, and a 31% drop in bounce rates, in initial tests with a select few ecommerce retailers. If you're running a medium-to-large sized Google Ads campaign, it's worth taking a look.

To say implementing AMP is extremely technically involved would be an understatement — it's something that should only be handled by the deft hands of a highly skilled web developer, and beyond the scope of this book.

But the potential upside in sales make it worth a look for medium-to-large campaigns. You can forward the official documentation by Google below to your web developer to see if it can be done, and read up on Accelerated Mobile Pages, in the "Google's Algorithm Updates" bonus chapter later in this book.

How to Use AMP With Google Ads - Google Ads
https://support.google.com/google-ads/answer/7495018

FURTHER GOOGLE ADS RESOURCES.

If you want to delve deeper into the pay-per-click rabbit-hole, the resources below are a great starting point for anyone starting out with pay-per-click advertising:

Ultimate Guide to Google AdWords - Perry Marshall

The *Ultimate Guide to Google Adwords* by Perry Marshall is often the starting point for many professionals starting out with PPC. Offers a great overview of Google Ads and delves into the inner game of successful Googel Ads campaigns. Great for beginners, but for more advanced techniques check out the following resources.

Advanced Google AdWords - Brad Geddes

If you want to be a pay-per-click guru, then look no further than this fantastic guide to advanced Google Ads management, great for both agencies and business owners running their own campaigns. Brad Geddes' magnum opus on advanced Google Ads pay-per-click advertising has been the secret treasure of many successful pay-per-click consultants, and readily available in Amazon and many other bookstores.

PPC Hero
https://www.ppchero.com/

PPC Hero is loaded with free advice on the latest Google Ads tricks and tips, but also covering fundamental pay-per-click methods that never change. Updated regularly.

Google Ads Blog
https://blog.google/products/ads/
Google's official blog for Google Ads. Great for the latest
Google Ads news direct from the horse's mouth.

That brings us to the end of the last bonus chapter of SEO
2020, and almost to the end of the book. Make sure you
download the SEO checklist available on the following
page as well as read through the final chapter for some
final tips in ensuring your overall success in ranking high
in the search results.

BONUS: 50 POINT SEO CHECKLIST PDF DOWNLOAD INSTRUCTIONS.

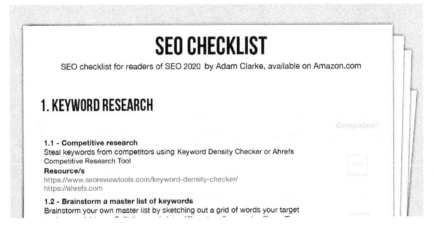

DOWNLOAD THE FREE SEO CHECKLIST

We've created an extensive SEO checklist so you can more easily improve your visibility in search engines in step-by-step format, as a small thank you for reading this book. It covers the following areas:

- Keyword research and finding the right keywords for your site, which tools to use, where to start, and so on...
- On-page optimization basics, optimizing keywords.
- Social media and web analytics setup tips.

- All technical areas covered in the book in an easy to understand step-by-step format, and much more...

WHERE TO ACCESS THE COMPLIMENTARY CHECKLIST.

The SEO checklist is available at the following url. https://www.simpleeffectiveness.com/seo-checklist

After downloading the checklist, make sure you remember to finish reading through the last chapter of the book for some final thoughts and tips on making your SEO campaigns successful.

FINAL THOUGHTS & TIPS.

WE'VE COVERED A LOT OF GROUND.

This book was written in a positive, light and conversational style in the hope of making a sometimes-difficult topic readable for readers from any background. At the same time, if you've read all the way to the finish line, you've covered a lot of ground, including:

- The basics of how Google works.
- Google's ranking factors.
- Keyword research.
- Improving your site's load speed.
- Optimizing keywords into your pages.
- Essentials for supporting mobile users.
- Optimizing user behavior.
- Link building, examples of beginner and advanced strategies.
- Social media and SEO.
- Web analytics basics.
- Common SEO problems and solutions and troubleshooting.
- Local SEO essentials.
- Targeting rich snippets and structured data.
- Steps for securing your website with HTTPS encryption.
- Google updates, RankBrain, HTTP/2, FRED, Hawk, and several others

- Recent updates such as the Google's BERT update and new guidelines on Nofollow tags.
- Staying ahead of future updates.
- Basics for Google Ads campaigns.
... and much more.

Congratulations on being a positive and proactive reader and finishing this book! The knowledge we've covered is more than enough to get started in SEO. It's also enough to increase rankings, traffic and sales if you already have moderate levels of success.

Don't forget why we learn SEO in the first place, details are important, but don't get bogged down in them. I often see many readers, business owners and marketers lost in endless articles, forums and blog posts on SEO and not making any progress with their projects or goals.

If there is one thing I want you to take away from this book, it isn't an appetite for details. I want you to finish this book with a propensity to action. Of all the readers I encounter, the most successful are those with a positive and proactive attitude, who put their new knowledge into action.

Remember, what matters most is you optimize your site well enough to beat competitors, make sales and grow your business. If your site shows stronger signals to Google than competitors, you will win in the rankings. Most importantly, have fun with it, make it your own, be positive and proactive!

~

CORRECTIONS & FEEDBACK.

I want this book to be the best for all readers, which is why I'm open to feedback from readers, and use feedback in updates as much as possible. Even if you are unhappy for any reason, noticed a mistake, or want something included, give me a chance to fix it and email me at adamclarkeseobook@gmail.com. I'll be happy to hear from you!

WHAT TO DO NEXT.

Which one or two sections did you particularly enjoy in this book? If you would like me to write more books in this simple and easy to understand format, please put up some stars, a review and any information on anything you particularly enjoyed on Amazon. Let other readers know what's in store for them. Just a small moment of your time will make my day.

https://bit.ly/seo-2020-book

- Adam Clarke

CPSIA information can be obtained
at www.ICGtesting.com
Printed in the USA
BVHW040207230320
575712BV00019B/1975